A Tale of Two Airfields

RAF Ashbourne & RAF Darley Moor

Noel J. Ryan & Chris Percy
Edited by Alison Walster

Published by:
WildTrack Publishing
Venture House
105 Arundel Street
Sheffield
S1 2NT

ISBN 978-1-904098-05-8

Cover image: No. 55 Course, RAF Ashbourne 1944 in front of one of 42 OTU's Albermarles (via Kath Howes).

ACKNOWLEDGEMENTS

The authors would like to express their thanks and appreciation to the following people and organisations for their help in the research of this book.

A. J. Jackson Collection; Brooklands Collection, Weybridge, Surrey; National Archives, Kew, Surrey; Royal Air Force Museum, Hendon; U. S. Department of Defense; Eileen Carlton (Secretary Irvin Caterpillar Club/Airborne Systems Canada Ltd.); Alan Clark (Peak District Air Accident Research Group); Brian Evans; Irma Esparzo (Airborne Systems, Santa Ana, USA); Daniel Fishman; Richard Flagg; Malcolm Giddings; Kath Howes; Steve Johnson (Cyberheritage.co.uk); Tony Lack (Flt. Sgt., RAF, Ret'd.); Simon Martin; Richard McLachlan; Eddie McBride; Don Midgley (ex-28 Maintenance Unit); Eddie Nelson (Darley Moor M.C.R.R.C); Stan Percy; Ken Rusby; Chris Russell; Len Simm; David J. Smith; Elliott Smock (Whitley Restoration Project); Steve Stancall (ex-28 Maintenance Unit); Paul Stanley (Peak Gateway Caravan Park); Mr. & Mrs Stevens; Dave Stubley (Lincolnshire Aircraft Recovery Group); Alison Walster; John and Gill Watson; Jeremy Wickins; Gerry Williams.

RAF Ashbourne and RAF Darley Moor – General Location

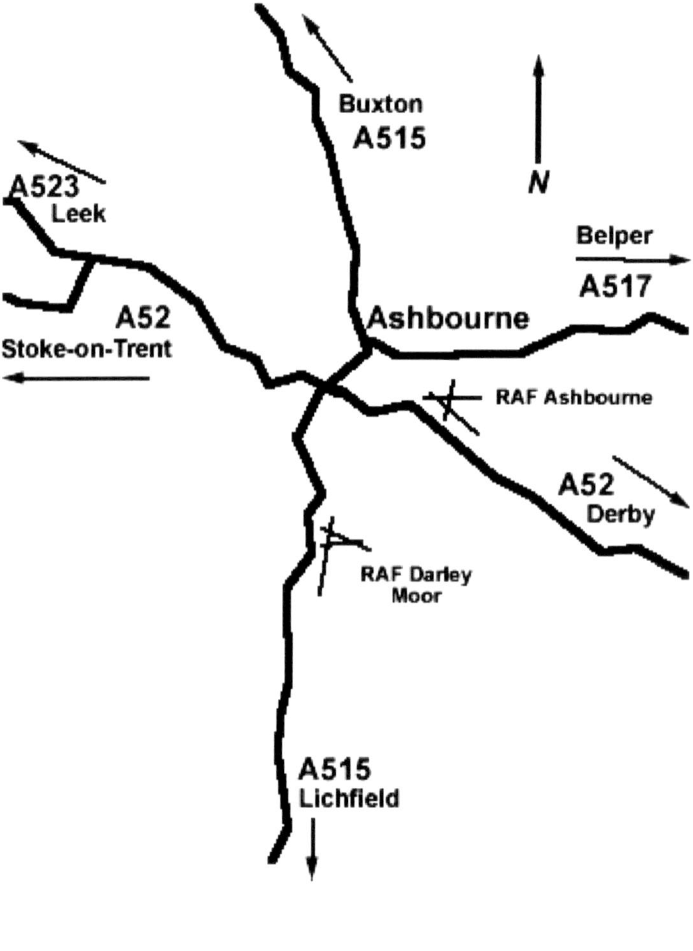

FOREWORD

FLIGHT SERGEANT TONY LACK RAF (RET'D.)

The Russian geographer, Mikhaylov, wrote "*The lines on the map are the handwriting of history*" and, during the 1940s, many new lines appeared on the map of Ashbourne and its surroundings.

These marked an airfield and its nearby satellite, Darley Moor and the many other dispersed sites needed to service the airfields and the needs of the airmen and airwomen stationed there, ensuring the efficiency of both these Royal Air Force Stations. Living quarters, sick quarters, transport workshops, air raid shelters and the many buildings needed on the airfield itself; hangars, crew rooms, storage areas and workshops. Elsewhere there was a large instructional site and an extensive communal site with messes, a gymnasium, cinema and other recreational buildings, many of which are still there and very well maintained as part of the Gateway Caravan Park.

In older peoples' memories there would be the impact on the town itself, the surrounding villages and farms all of whom had to live with the constant noise of heavy twin-engined aircraft practicing their take offs and landings and cross country flights all day and all night - weather permitting.

The purpose of both of these airfields was for Operational Training, a vital and final stage in aircrew training as this was the point at which different aircrew members came together to form that important unit, a crew, to prepare them for operational combat.

The handwriting of these "*lines on the map*" in this area of Derbyshire is expertly read and explained to us in this book by two enthusiastic researchers who have done their work mainly "on site" and also, unusually, from the air. It is a valuable piece of local history.

TONY LACK
Ex-Flight Sergeant, RAF
Ashbourne
2006

BEGINNINGS

The Coming of the Airfields

Great care was taken in the selection of sites for military airfield construction. This was especially so during what is termed the *RAF Expansion Period* of the 1930s, which accelerated during the Munich Crisis of 1938.

Generally, most airfield sites followed a standard pattern of layout, both in runways and architecture, with many of the buildings (especially those for the higher ranks) being of a neo-Georgian style and very impressive. There were, naturally, a few modifications which were dictated by both function and topography but the majority of the airfields at the time were laid out with permanent buildings, both technical and accommodation, in a tightly knit group alongside the grass-surfaced flying strips.

The grass runways commonly found on these airfields was to become a problem with the onset of war, as aircraft size and all-up weights began to increase. The need for hard-surfaced runways was becoming a necessity, thereby influencing the choice of location for those stations where the heavier bombers would be based. The acknowledgment of the heavier types was also reflected in the orders given by the Air Ministry, in 1941, to increase main runway lengths at many then existing and subsequently, all new heavy bomber stations from 1400 yards (1280 metres) to 2000 yards (1828 meters).

A priority at this time, although not an overwhelming one, was given to the construction of bomber airfields as a means of taking the fight back to the enemy. To qualify a site as suitable for a prospective aerodrome, certain criteria were laid down by the Air Ministry Aerodromes Board during the late 1930s.

The stipulations included (such items) that an airfield site should be free from natural and man-made obstructions including trees and buildings, be at least five miles from a neighbouring airfield site, have good drainage and to reduce the hazards of low cloud or fog, be not more than 600 feet (183 metres) above sea level (ASL).

The surveying of both the Ashbourne and Darley Moor sites was undertaken at a time when official doctrines could be interpreted slightly differently from those described, due to the pressing necessities of the conflict during 1941 - airfields were needed urgently. As a result, the areas chosen to house the airfields were in fact *less* than five miles from their nearest neighbours (Ashbourne and Darley Moor are 2.7 miles (4.3 Km) apart from their respective geographical centres). Both sites only just qualify with regards to altitude, with Ashbourne being at the prescribed limit of 600 feet (183 metres) ASL and Darley Moor, 580 feet (176 metres) ASL. Both sites also had obstructions to contend with, notably local housing and farms and at least two local dwellings were to suffer as a direct result of accidents during Ashbourne's career and will be covered later. The local man-made obstructions notwithstanding, there was also the high ground in the vicinity. Many of the local hills, (one of the highest being Madge Hill, about five miles to the north-east of both sites, reaches 977 feet (297 metres) ASL), are on a parity with both airfields' altitude. The high ground also presented some problematic local weather conditions, which would later come to hinder the training programme and flying in general from both airfields.

Both sites were surveyed for suitability in early 1941 and by the Spring of the same year, construction had begun at RAF

Ashbourne by principal contractors Lehane, McKenzie & Shand. The airfield followed the standard pattern for what is known as a Class-A bomber airfield, with three intersecting runways surrounded by a perimeter track, along with the Technical Site and accommodation and ancillary buildings in the surrounding countryside. Ashbourne's runways were set on a limestone hardcore of locally quarried material and laid by hand as stone setts or 'pobs'.

The area soon became something of an adventure playground and one correspondent, Gerry Williams, clearly remembers 'helping' the Irish labourers associated with the construction gangs working on the project. He also remembers that after the laying of the pobs, came a second layer of limestone pea gravel, used to infill between the pobs and act as a consolidating medium for the underlay. This was topped off with a concrete surface. After much experimentation with runway surfaces elsewhere, both Ashbourne and Darley Moor received a final skim of concrete and wood chip. This combination was proven to reduce reflectivity when the surface was wet, aiding camouflage and also to provide grip, although aircraft tyre wear was found to be an issue at many stations. During the construction of Ashbourne airfield many local children could regularly be seen 'assisting' the civilian contractors with their work. Part of the main runway owes its existence, in a small way at least, to the toils of Mr. Williams. Many years later, a little wiser now, he would return to claim part of his work after sections of the runways were grubbed out and later form part of his garden wall and patio!

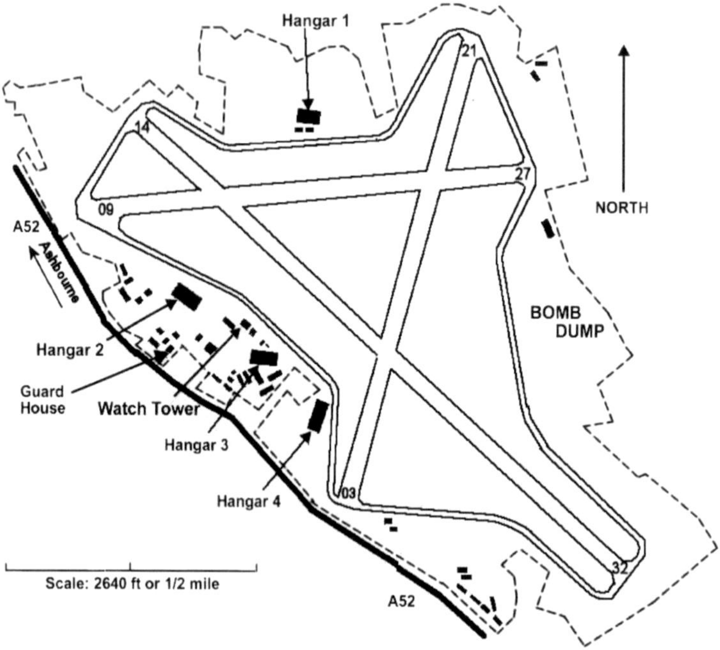

Figure 1: Airfield & Technical Site general arrangement.
(adapted by C. Percy from A/M Drawing Number 1116/45)

RAF ASHBOURNE
Opened: 1942
Closed: 1954

Formation: 38 Group

Unit(s): 42 OTU (1942-46); 28 Maintenance Unit (1950-54)

Runway Surface: Concrete & woodchip

Hangars: four T2

Affiliated Airfields: Darley Moor

Current Use: Industry & agriculture

Runway Number	*Heading*	*Direction*	*Length*	*Width*
01/04	$310^{o}/130^{o}$ (31/13)	SSW/NNE	1400 yards (1280m)	50 yards (45m)
02/05	$270^{o}/090^{o}$ (27/09)	W/E	1400 yards (128 m)	50 yards (45m)
03/06	$320^{o}/140^{o}$ (32/14)	NW/SE	2000 yards (1828m)	50 yards (45m)

Table 1: Ashbourne's Runways (adapted from Willis & Holliss, 1987)

The runways were surrounded by an encircling perimeter track 50 feet (15 metres) wide, to which were connected thirty, 125 foot (38 metre) diameter 'frying-pan' dispersals, so-called because of their appearance in plan view. The construction of the runways raised the question of obstructions near the airfield site. At least three dwellings were demolished; Tom Gadsby, being one such resident making way for a significant landscape change. The houses in question were along the northern side of the A52, which forms the south-western boundary of the main airfield site, opposite Preston's Garage, which still exists to this day. Also, a house nearby to Preston's had to undergo the unusual modification of having its upper floor removed. The reason for this molestation was that these properties were directly beneath the flight path of runway 27/09.

Other local landscape changes included the closure of Lady Hole Lane at the south-eastern end of the site, to make way for the main north-west/south-east runway (32/14). Properties along this road now found themselves having dispersals at the ends of their gardens! Another victim was an older property, Roadmeadow Farm, which was perched on the escarpment immediately adjacent to the A52, across the road from the main airfield site. Again it was an obstruction, deemed to be in such a position as to hinder the approach and departure of aircraft, so it too was demolished. No such action was required for runway 31/13, whose flight path was clear of obstructions.

The airfield site contained a total of ninety-six buildings, ranging from four T2 Hangars, measuring 239' 7" long by 130' 10" wide (72.8 metres by 39 metres), to Air Ministry Drawing Number 8254/40, to the workshops and technical support buildings, blast shelters, bomb stores and fuzing points, squadron and flight offices, the Control (or Watch) Tower, latrines and even a salt store.

Fortunately, no demolition was required for the dispersed, communal, instructional and living sites at Ashbourne. As was common practice by this time in the War, these were situated some distance away from the parent airfield site: airfield sites differed from their pre-war Expansion Period counterparts in that, unlike these aerodromes, camouflage and dispersal were the order of the day. This minimised the potential damage from air attack, being less conspicuous from the air. Once the airfield site construction was under-way, it was up to the Unit Construction Company to take over the work on these dispersed sites. The areas associated with Ashbourne were located to the south and south-west of the airfield and utilised natural features as cover. Masked somewhat by the undulating contours of the landscape south of the airfield plateau, some of these sites were located in or near existing parcels of woodland or near suitably dense coverts, the relicts of both woodland and buildings may still be seen today.

Distributed over eighteen separate locations at RAF Ashbourne, these sites comprised everything from the Women's Auxiliary Air Force (WAAF) Dormitory site, Station Sick Quarters, an Instructional site, the High Frequency Direction Finding station (H.F.D.F., known in Air Force parlance as *huff-duff*), and the Station Sewage Works. All of these buildings were classed as "temporary", with a variety of materials and to a number of official drawing patterns. Commonly seen were the brick and concrete-rendered huts, along with Nissen huts with their characteristic corrugated steel coverings and Laing or L-type wooden huts.

There was nothing classical about the construction of these facilities for souls living, working and flying from here, unlike the Expansion Period, permanent structures of the 1930s. The buildings were designed to be quick and easy to erect; functional, utilitarian, austere.

	Officers	*Senior NCOs*	*Other Ranks*	*Total*
RAF	171	454	1472	2097
WAAF	10	16	432	458
TOTAL	181	470	1904	2555

Table 2: Ashbourne's personnel compliment (as of December 1944) (adapted from Hollis & Williss, 1987)

Whilst Ashbourne was being considered as a bomber airfield, thoughts turned to the need for satellite stations. Originally, Ashbourne was to have two such locations associated with it; Darley Moor and Church Broughton, also in Derbyshire. Ultimately, Church Broughton was to become a significant training airfield in its own right, leaving Darley Moor to be chosen as the single satellite airfield for Ashbourne.

Work was commenced here in mid-1942 by contractors Monk's of Warrington, the principal sub-contractor being Bradshaw Brothers of Leicester, who undertook the levelling of the site. The father of Ashbourne resident John Watson was a member of the levelling team at Darley Moor working for Bradshaw's as a tractor driver, preparing the ground for the construction of the runways and perimeter track.

John Watson's father aboard his tractor during the early phases of preparation work at Darley Moor,1942. (via John & Gill Watson)

John Watson's father (right) and colleague, Darley Moor, 1942. (via John & Gill Watson)

As with Ashbourne, Darley Moor was constructed to Class-A bomber airfield standard, with three intersecting runways. At this stage of both sites' development, it was envisaged that they would be front-line airfields, housing operational heavy bomber squadrons. Consequently, the airfield site comprised the usual runways, encircling perimeter track, and Technical Site.

Again, local obstructions were an issue, in this case the hazard was the village of Wyaston, which lay just 300 yards (275 metres) from the threshold of the east-west runway (27/09). However, there is no evidence to suggest that recommendations be made for the entire village to be flattened! The building of the airfield did entail the closure of a minor road linking the A515, to the west of the airfield, to the hamlets of Hales Green and Yeaveley, to the south-east of the site.

The runways were linked by a 50 foot wide (15 metre) perimeter track. Off-shot from this, at intervals, were twenty-seven, 125 foot (38 metre) diameter frying pan hard standings for aircraft parking. The Technical Site was built to the west and north of the airfield site, alongside the A515. Only one hangar was constructed, a single T2, adjacent to the south-eastern perimeter track, with the bomb store located behind it in fields a little further to the east. Associated sites alongside Windmill Lane, with the junction of the A515 to the west, included the Headquarters Site, which contained the Operations Block and the Instructional Site. The latter included the Bombing Teacher and Turret Instructional building, classrooms and the Link Trainer building, which contained two of these pioneering flight simulators.

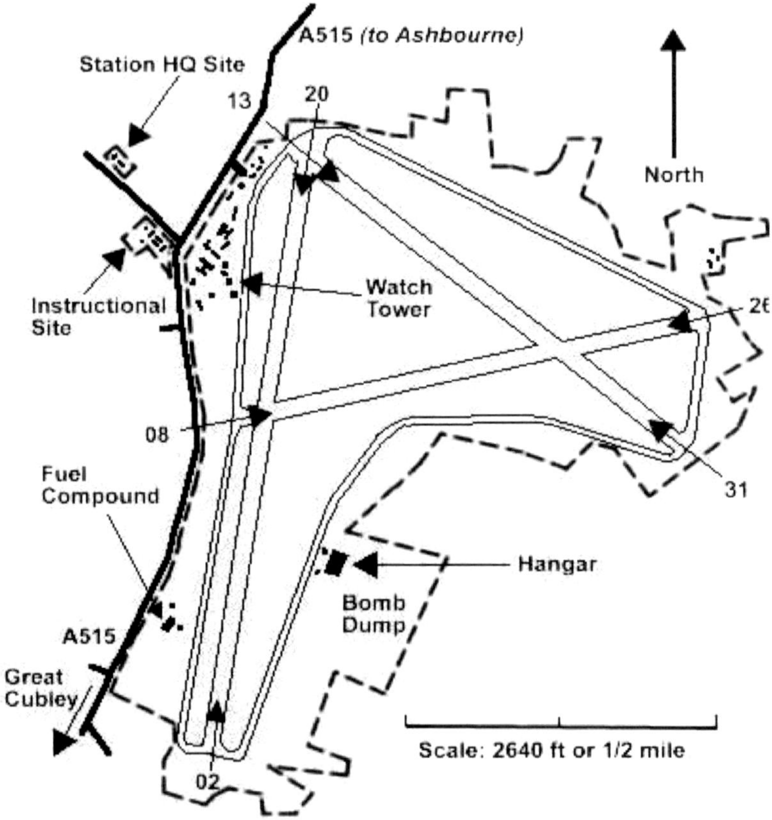

Figure 2: Airfield & Technical Site general arrangement (adapted by C. Percy from A/M Drawing Number 330/45)

RAF DARLEY MOOR
Opened: 1942
Closed: 1945

Formation: 38 Group

Unit(s): 42 OTU (1942-46); 28 Maintenance Unit (1950-54)

Runway Surface: Concrete & wood chip

Hangars: one T2

Affiliated Airfields: Ashbourne

Current Use: Motorsport, agriculture and light aviation

Runway Number	*Heading*	*Direction*	*Length*	*Width*
1	$200^{O}/020^{O}$ (20/02)	N/S	1800 yards (1646 m)	50 yards (45 m)
2	$269^{O}/089^{O}$ (27/09)	E/W	1400 yards (1280 m)	50 yards (45 m)
3	$319^{O}/139^{O}$ (32/14)	NW/SE	1400 yards (1280 m)	50 yards (45 m)

Table 3: Darley Moor's Runways (adapted from Hollis & Williss, 1987)

The dispersed and living accommodation was spread to the north-west of the airfield and the A515 over seven sites. Again, everything was catered for, from dining rooms, barbers and hairdressers, sick quarters and a grocery store (usually stocking local produce). All were included to make the station as self-sufficient as possible.

	Officers	*Senior NCOs*	*Other Ranks*	*Total*
RAF	60	267	735	1062
WAAF	8	40	135	183
TOTAL	68	307	870	1245

Table 4: Darley Moor's personnel compliment (as of December 1944) (adapted from Hollis & Williss, 1987)

Much of this accommodation was again hidden by natural cover, the broad-leaved woodland providing excellent camouflage around the dispersed sites, notably Gorse Covert to the west (the Station Headquarters), the woods around Collycroft Farm (Site No. 3) and Gravel Pit Covert (Site No. 4), both to the north-west. To the immediate east of the A515, on the airfield site, was sited one of the fuel compounds. This particular facility provided bulk fuel storage for 48,000 gallons of aviation fuel.

A visit was made to Ashbourne by Air Marshall Arthur T. Harris (Commander-in-Chief, Bomber Command), during its construction to view the progress and it gave him cause for concern. It was becoming clear that because of the geographical and meteorological constraints of the site, Ashbourne would not, after all, be able to fulfill its role as a front line heavy bomber station. Although rejected as an offensive bomber airfield from such a high level, this rejection decision was not solely that of Harris. The existing and proposed infrastructure present at both Ashbourne and Darley Moor airfields would make them both ideally suited to that of Operational Training Units (OTUs), catering for heavy aircraft. Consequently, when opened, both sites came under the administration of No. 92 (Training) Group Bomber Command, it was the new 81 OTU which started to form at Ashbourne, with Darley Moor as the satellite station. Due to a geographical reorganisation within Bomber Command the few service personnel found themselves on the move again. This embryonic echelon was to form the OTU properly after being transferred to Whitchurch Heath (also known as Tilstock), Shropshire (September 1942), whereupon it began to receive its compliment of aircraft

Eggington Hall in 1977 (M. L. Giddings).

Ashbourne and Darley Moor now came under the control of 93 (Training) Group, the Group's Headquarters were to be located at Eggington Hall in Derbyshire.

Further changes in Royal Air Force administration now decreed that the two stations would no longer be part of the Bomber Command training programme. Rather, they would now be part of 70 Group, Army Co-Operation Command, allowing the Army to undertake practice in dealing with low-flying aircraft and receiving supply drops. One unit which was already under this Command was 42 OTU, at that time based at Andover in Hampshire which was moved officially to its new home of Ashbourne in October 1942. Here they remained (carrying out training duties which will be described in detail later), until the announcement that 70 Group was to be transferred from Army Co-operation to the Air Defence of Great Britain (ADGB). With this switch of Command, Ashbourne, Darley Moor and the incumbent 42 OTU were now transferred to No. 38 Group. Although a Fighter Training Group, training continued in much the same vein - ground support and supply dropping, but slowly becoming more specialised, until the Group became an Airborne

Forces Support Group. Ashbourne was to be home to 'B' and 'C' Flights (or Squadrons, as they were to be known) and Darley Moor, 'A' Flight.

As the sole occupants of both stations, 42 OTU were to remain resident until the cessation of hostilities in Europe in 1945, with training gradually winding down in the preceding months before VE-Day, Tuesday, 8th May 1945. Both stations were then placed on a 'Care and Maintenance' footing until 1950, when 28 Maintenance Unit (MU), based at Buxton, began to utilise the runways and former bomb dumps of both stations for the storage and care of high explosive and other ordnance. This continued until 1954, when the sites were eventually disposed of.

THE AIRCRAFT

Whilst at Ashbourne and Darley Moor, 42 OTU flew a variety of aircraft which reflected the needs of such a unit. Many of the airmen passing through the doors of 42 OTU had earned their wings under the Empire Air Training Scheme (EATS) in the sunnier climes of South Africa, Australia, New Zealand and Canada. The scheme, starting in 1939, ensured clear, less crowded skies and good weather with no enemy intervention. On returning to UK shores, it was soon realised (by 1941) that crews needed acclimatising to flying in the European Theatre of Operations. Once posted to an OTU, not only was there the need for theatre training but also the need for a bringing together of the various flying trades; navigators, pilots, gunners, etc., and formed into units to train as a crew, ultimately on aircraft types similar to those of the front line, before being posted to an operational squadron.

One factor which the EATS was intended to mitigate against was the weather. The sunny, clear skies which the trainees experienced abroad were lacking in Britain. Due to the location and altitude of both airfields used by 42 OTU fog, low cloud, snow and rain, would all impede to some extent the training schedules.

It was not just the weather which would have an impact upon the training. The diverse number of aircraft found at OTUs reflected the refinement of the aircrew's trades but as was common with many other training establishments, the aircraft themselves were not always factory fresh examples. Indeed, some had already been in front line use for some time, often with more than one unit, before being relegated to training and 42 OTU was no exception with its influx of aircraft.

Whilst it is not the purpose of this book to give full histories of the aircraft concerned, the following pages at least give the reader some insight into the types flown by 42 OTU whilst at Ashbourne and Darley Moor. It highlights specific characteristics and details and also explains the roles in which they were employed whilst on duty with the Unit.

Bristol Blenheim

The mainstay aircraft of 42 OTU whilst at Andover was the Bristol Blenheim Mk. I. Originally designed as a fast, light commercial aircraft for routes over continental northern Europe from the UK, it was soon found to be ideally suited as a light bomber. Both in this variant and its fighter derivative (the Mk. If), the Blenheim carried out sterling service in the opening phases of World War 2 and was also a pioneer aircraft in the new art of night fighting, equipped with early Airborne Interception radar. It was realised that as a day bomber, it was vulnerable to the contemporary Luftwaffe fighter types, such as the Messerschmitt Bf109. That notwithstanding, the Blenheim continued in production as a front line aircraft but by late 1941, many were now being transferred into the training role.

Used for a variety of tasks, including pilot and navigator training, the Belnheim's used by 42 OTU were a small number of factory fresh Blenheim Mk I's, complimented by ex-front line aircraft, and at least seven of this variant found their way to the Derbyshire airfields when the move from RAF Andover occurred in 1942. This Mark of the type was, by November 1943, was being phased out by 42 OTU, either being transferred elsewhere or simply struck off charge and scrapped.

Bristol Blenheim 1f. (A. J. Jackson collection)

Overlapping the Blenheim Mk. Is at Ashbourne and Darley Moor were the later Blenheim Mk. IVs, along with a small number of the Blenheim Mk. Vs. With their characteristic longer, glazed nose extension, the Mk. IVs and Vs fulfilled much the same role as their predecessors; that of pilot and navigation training. As was the case with the Blenheim I, the proportion of 'second hand' airframes was slightly higher than those of new aircraft and consequently, serviceability was always an issue.

Engine failures, structural integrity and maintenance were the order of the day in what were undeniably over-worked aircraft and it is probable that many had exceeded their operational design life. The Blenheims soldiered on but the operability issue resulted in one too many incidents and forced the decision to withdraw the type entirely from the unit's manifest in August, 1943.

Bristol Blenheim Mk. V, RAF Museum, Hendon.
(Chris Percy, 1987)

Restored Blenheim Mk. V at Duxford (Richard E. Flagg)

ARMSTRONG WHITWORTH WHITLEY MK. V

Armstrong Whitworth Whitley Mk. V, in this case the prototype.
(via Elliott Smock, Whitley Restoration Project)

The Whitley had been in production and front line service since 1936 and the Whitley Mk. V was to serve in some numbers with 42 OTU. Previous Marks had already been part of the mainstay of Bomber Command. The Whitley Mk. V, appeared in 1938 and became the most widely produced variant and stalwart of many OTU's after its withdrawal from front line service. The earlier marks were powered by the Armstrong-Siddeley Tiger engine which proved to be under-powered and troublesome. This resulted in the fitment of the Roll-Royce Merlin IV power plant (the Whitley Mk. IV) and later the Merlin X, resulting in the Whitley Mk. V, which defined the type operated by 42 OTU. Apart from the engine modifications, the Whitley Mk. V also had a 15 inch (38 cm) rear fuselage extension, giving the rear gunner a wider field of view and fire.

By 1942, the Whitley had been withdrawn as a front line combat aeroplane but was now used in some quantities by numerous training establishments. In the case of 42 OTU, the rôles the aircraft initially performed were that of a gunnery trainer, supply drop and general navigation platform. As a trainer, the Whitley was found to be a stable and forgiving aircraft.

Whilst issues of serviceability dogged its career, it was found by the ground crews who serviced the type to be equally forgiving when it came to the maintenance schedule.

Although the type was already nearing obsolescence during 1941, early trials had been undertaken at the Royal Aircraft Establishment at Farnborough in this year into the feasibility of the Whitley airframe being used as a glider tug. Initially, the towing equipment was housed in the rear turret position but this was later moved to a more robust towing yoke underneath the fuselage, below the tail empennage. These trials continued for some time until, in October 1942, the first one, involving a Whitley and an Airspeed Horsa glider combination were carried out successfully. This occurrence would impact upon 42 OTU as, by 1943, after the transfer into 38 Group, it would see the unit and its Whitleys become heavily involved with the training of glider tug crews. The Whitley/Horsa combinations became a familiar sight over the Derbyshire countryside, especially in the months leading up to D-Day in 1944.

AIRSPEED OXFORD

Another training aircraft which was born out of a private civil venture, the Oxford was a direct descendant of the Airspeed Envoy light commercial of 1934. As with the Blenheim, it was found suitable for Royal Air Force service but this time it was directly admitted as an advanced multi-engined trainer in 1938. The type would not have been unfamiliar to the crews returning back to UK shores under EATS, as several hundred were employed at the training units abroad.

The Oxford operated in both the Mk. I and Mk. II variants whilst with 42 OTU. Externally, there was little to difference between them, apart from the fitting of an Armstrong Whitworth dorsal turret to the Mk. I, mounting one .303 inch (7.7mm) Vickers K machine gun, along with a basic bomb bay. This variant, powered by Armstrong Siddeley Cheetah X radial engines was an all round trainer, fitted with dual controls, a Sperry blind flying instrument panel and usually operated with a crew of three or four. Along with the pilot, the mix of personnel might include a second pilot, a navigator, a radio operator or camera operator. The latter would record, on film, the results of bombing or gunnery training flights for analysis back at base.

Airspeed A.S. 10 Oxford II.

With the mid-upper turret omitted, the Oxford II was intended solely for the training of pilots, navigators and radio operators. Other than the removal of the turret, the airframe was unchanged and retained the same power plants. The Oxford served with 42 OTU from the unit's inception to the cessation of hostilities in 1945.

AVRO ANSON

The Avro Anson was yet another aircraft derived from a light commercial aircraft, the Avro 652; the militarised version was known as the Avro 652A Anson. Entering service in 1936, the Anson was initially used in a front line role by Coastal Command, patrolling UK waters and Channel shipping lanes.

As war grew increasingly likely, the Anson was used as a stop-gap bomber by Bomber Command during the RAF Expansion Period of 1937, around the time of the Munich Crisis. It performed this task until the heavier, purpose-built types, such as the Whitley and the Vickers Wellington, began to come off of the production lines in any useful numbers in the following year or two.

Avro Anson, Imperial War Museum, Duxford.
(Noel J Ryan, 2004)

Although used as a front line combat aircraft just prior to and including the opening stages of the War, the primary function of the Anson was that of an advanced trainer and it had begun serving with Elementary and Reserve Flying Training Schools in 1936. The majority of service aircrew would have, at some time, become familiar with the Anson, as it was also used overseas in some quantities under the EATS. In the UK, at most OTUs, the Anson compliment was usually four or five aircraft at any one time, although an audit of 42 OTU in 1943 revealed 16 on strength. The usual rounds of aircraft transfer, along with accidents and write-offs kept these number stable. The Ansons initially used by 42 OTU also migrated from RAF Andover and were perhaps the longest serving type with the unit, being employed as pilot, navigator and radio operator trainer from 18th July 1941 to 20th March 1945.

WESTLAND LYSANDER MK. III

When 42 OTU was formed, its role, under the administration of 70 Group, was that of Army co-operation and as such, it operated a small number of Lysanders. First flown in 1936, the Lysander was purpose-built for the task of Army liaison and was also used for training ground troops to contend with low flying enemy aircraft, giving them something to shoot at (with blanks of course!). Its superb low speed, low-level handling characteristics made it ideal for the job. Of course, its remarkable ability to take-off and land in confined areas and fields made it ideal for the illustrious Special Operations Executive (S.O.E) Special Duties Squadrons' incursions into occupied Europe later in the war, undertaking many clandestine flights in support of Resistance movements, secret agent drops and collections and occasionally, repatriating downed RAF crews evading capture.

Westland Lysander Mk. III, Imperial War Museum, Duxford.. This aircraft wears the camouflage and markings of 161 (Special Duties) Sqn (Noel J Ryan. 2005)

The Lysander variant with 42 OTU was the Mk. III. Powered by an 870 hp Bristol Mercury engine, the aircraft was used by the unit from 1941, progressing from the Army co-operation role as, when group changes occurred, to that of a target tug. Having a distinctive appearance in flight with its high-mounted wing, with 42 OTU it was made even more distinguishable with the undersides of the aircraft being painted in black and yellow stripes, denoting its role as a target tug. The Lysander was phased out of service by 42 OTU in late 1944.

Miles Martinet

Miles Martinet target tug. The wind-driven winch gear is clearly visible below the cockpit canopy.

The Miles Martinet was the first RAF aircraft specifically designed for the purpose of towing airborne targets (drogues). The aircraft was designed by Phillips & Powis and there was already a healthy pedigree of both light civilian sports aircraft and military trainers to emerge from the Miles stable and the Martinet was part of this succession. The airframe was based upon the already successful Miles Master advanced trainer. Powered by a similar engine to the Lysander, a Bristol Mercury, the airframe differed from the Master by being strengthened to cope with the stresses of towing targets; a slightly longer nose, higher-placed cockpit and a slightly larger wingspan. The airframe itself was constructed largely of wood, being a spruce frame covered with a plywood skin. The drougues and towing gear were contained in a fairing beneath the fuselage and were powered by an external, wind-driven winch.

The Martinet first appeared in April 1942 and was immediately put into service as a target tug with many Operational Training Units. Number 42 OTU operated this sturdy little utilitarian aircraft from the time it was introduced until the Unit's disbandment in 1945.

SUPERMARINE SPITFIRE

Fighter affiliation exercises were commonplace at OTUs and 42 was no exception. As part of the training syllabus, a small number of Spitfires (and Hurricanes) were used to train air gunners in the art of dealing with attacking fighter aircraft.

Supermarine Spitfire Mk.Ia, RAF Museum, Hendon. (Chris Percy, 1987)

As mentioned previously, many of the aircraft operated by 42 OTU were 'second hand' and this is amply illustrated by one Spitfire which served with the unit:

"*Spitfire Mk. I, X4387: First Flight, 07/09/40; Maintenance Unit, 09/09/40; 234 Sqn, 10/09/40; Flying Accident Category 2, 19/11/40; Morris Motors, Oxford (no date); 306 Sqn, 06/10/41; 52 OTU, 03/01/42; Accident, Category E, 08/09/43; 42 OTU, 03/05/44; Struck Off Charge, 17/01/45.*"

(Morgan & Shacklady, 1987)

Clearly the aircraft had led an eventful life before reaching its final destination in Derbyshire. Suffering a Category 2 flying accident and latterly, a Category E incident (which under normal circumstances may have necessitated a write-off), this hard-worked and long-lived Spitfire almost managed to reach end of hostilities. The incidents which resulted in the damage are not available.

Armstrong Whitworth Albemarle

Whilst the initial phases of training were undertaken by the variety of types already operated by 42 OTU, after the transfer to 38 Group and the change in rôle to that of transport training, one aircraft was to become synonymous with the unit, Ashbourne and Darley Moor – the Armstrong Whitworth Albemarle.

Designed as a medium bomber by the Bristol Aeroplane Company, it was passed over to Armstrong Whitworth for further development as a reconnaissance bomber. Like its more famous contemporary, the de Havilland Mosquito, the Albemarle was built largely of wood, principally a spruce frame with a stressed plywood skin. This resulted in an airframe which was prone to delays in manufacture due to the disparate nature of the sub-contractors involved, many of which were wood-working specialists, skilled in the art of furniture and cabinet making, with workshops scattered away from the main assembly plant at the principal sub-contractor's, A. W. Hawklsey's, in Gloucester.

Armstrong Whitworth Albemarle P1442 which served with 42OTU.
(via Len Simm)

These delays in manufacture and ultimately, production, meant that the type was almost obsolete for its intended function by the time full scale production and deliveries began in late 1940. Consequently, the Royal Air Force made the decision to use the aircraft in a transport role, as Special Transports and Glider Tugs. It was these roles which would dictated the Mark number designations – ST and GT, and 42 OTU would see a quantity of both of these types pass through its hangar doors. Interestingly, it was the only domestically-produced aircraft in RAF service in World War 2 with a tricycle, nose-wheeled arrangement (many US, Lend-Lease aircraft such as the North American B-25 Mitchell were nose-wheeled types).

Powered by two 1, 590 hp Bristol Hercules XI radial engines, the Albemarle was slightly underpowered for its all-up weight of 36,500lb (16,556 kg). These power plants were prone to over-heating, a fault which was never technically cured, although an attempt was made by the risky expedient of raising of the recommended cylinder-head operating temperatures from 280 deg C to 300 deg C. This was a decision which would have later ramifications.

The Albemarle was able to carry out the duties assigned to it competently enough but some of the aircraft's handling characteristics left it reportedly unpopular with its pilots: low speed handling, single-engined flight and stalling being particularly troublesome areas of the flight envelope. Although Armstrong Whitworth test pilot John Grierson gave it a clean bill of health, he reported that "...[the aircraft] *has no virtues or vices...*", describing it as 'average'.

The shortcomings of the types flying abilities in some situations could be directly attributed to many incidents in which they were involved, a number of which were combined with engine failure at critical moments, especially at take-off and landing, or in bad weather.

The Marks of Albemarle used by 42 OTU were outwardly similar, with refinements made to the interiors to reflect the purpose for which they would serve. Although several variants of the Albemarle were to eventually come off of the production lines, only two were to be found at Ashbourne and Darley Moor; the GT and the ST and their sub-series.

AIRSPEED HORSA

First flown in 1941, the Airspeed A.S. 51 Horsa was designed and built as a heavy assault glider to Air Ministry Specification Number X26/40. The airframe was constructed of wood and production was carried out by Airspeed's, with sub-contracted production by Austin Motors and furniture makers Harris Lebus, the nose sections being constructed by Bolton-Paul Aircraft Ltd. In total, 3655 Horsa airframes were built. One of the largest gliders to be used by the Allied Forces in World War Two, it was able to lift a considerable load (15, 250 lb/6920 kg), be towed at 127 mph and glide at 100 mph (204 km/h / 160 km/h respectively).

Airspeed Horsa. (A. J. Jackson collection)

The glider was of a tricycle undercarriage layout with a nose-wheel. These units were built to be jettisoned if necessary, the Horsa being able to land on an inbuilt skid arrangement, which was normally retracted below the fuselage. The aircraft also had good handling characteristics, especially aided by the large wing flaps which, when extended, allowed steep but rapid descents into confined spaces. This feature was put to very good use in many of the airborne operations upon which it was ultimately deployed, for example the assaults on *Pegasus Bridge* in the early hours of 6th June, 1944 and the ill-fated *Operation Market Garden* Arnhem raid of September 17th, 1944. Both of these operations involved crews from 42 OTU who had graduated to the front-line Squadrons of 38 Group flying the Albemarle.

Whilst 42 OTU were actively training pilots and crews to tow gliders, so far research has only revealed two examples of the aircraft which were directly issued to 42 OTU (DP799, transferred to No. 1 Heavy Glider Storage Unit and LJ139, transferred to 21 Heavy Glider Conversion Unit). Many of the assault gliders used in the large operations in the latter half of the Second World War were rarely issued to the Squadrons involved. The gliders were normally held in storage until operational requirements saw their issue to front line units.

The aircraft of 42 OTU were to be seen on a very regular basis over northern Derbyshire, Staffordshire and the surrounding districts. Pilot training and navigational exercises would see the aircraft on two, three or four hour trips deep into the Midlands, over east Anglia and Lincolnshire as well as over the Irish Sea. Closer to their home bases, many aircraft were also to be seen over the locally assigned ranges. These were Kinder Scout in the Peak District, about thirty miles to the north-north-west of Ashbourne and Carsington, five miles to the north-east.

Kinder Scout would witness live firing exercises, with the drogue-towing Lysanders and Martinets providing the means for the air gunners in the Oxfords, Ansons, Blenheims and Whitleys to master their skills. At the site of what is now Carsington Reservoir was the location for the practice dropping of supply canisters. Here the Oxfords, Whitleys and Albemarle's could been seen, plying their trades in preparation for the crew's later duties which were to become so vital in some of the most significant airborne and airborne-assisted operations of World War 2.

It was with these aircraft and these tasks that 42 OTU, RAF Ashbourne and RAF Darley Moor would come together as a training establishment and these airfields were to become home to many hundreds of aircrew and their ground support for the next three years.

A CHANGE OF PLAN

Ashbourne airfield was officially handed over to the Air Ministry on 10th July 1942, although RAF personnel had been in residence for some weeks preceding this. The site was, at this point, still in an unfinished state with many of the accommodation and Technical Site buildings still to be fully completed. For a while, the first arrivals had to go into the town of Ashbourne for meals. It was, nonetheless, usable as an airfield, with completion taking place, as with so many wartime airfields, alongside the day to day operations. Despite the airfield being designed and built as a Class-A heavy bomber station, it was unsuitable for this purpose. With successive changes in administration, circumstances would dictate the role Ashbourne would now serve; to train air crews for Bomber Command for the campaign in mainland Europe.

Initially, 92 (Training) Group Bomber Command under Air Commodore H. A. Haines DFC, was to administer Ashbourne and Darley Moor. It was planned to create and base a new unit, 81 OTU, at Ashbourne under 92 (Training) Group Bomber Command, which would be equipped with Vickers Wellingtons and the intended compliment to begin with was twenty seven aircraft, including two reserves. Ultimately, it was envisaged that 81 OTU would have nearly sixty Wellingtons based at Ashbourne, although many of these would have subsequently been based at Darley Moor, once that station was operational.

An advance party of men and equipment now arrived as the embryonic 81 OTU took shape and was officially formed on the 10th July 1942. Apart from the odd visiting aircraft conveying various high ranking officers, none of the Wellingtons had so far arrived. The first Commanding Officer was Squadron Leader (Sqn. Ldr.) Boston, who took up residence. He was accompanied by a Warrant Officer (W/O), three Non-Commissioned Officers (NCOs) and thirty other ranks, who began the task of administering and coordinating the setting up of the OTU. A mass of motor vehicles was also arriving on a near daily basis; tractors, petrol bowsers, ambulances and fire tenders, plus all of the accoutrements needed to start a flying unit. All this aroused much interest and speculation amongst the locals who, keen to see what was happening in their neighbourhood, gathered to watch the new arrivals.

This local interest naturally extended to the young lads of the area, who would regularly make attempts to access the site. Once the airfield had been handed over to the RAF, this ceased and their unofficial playground became off-limits more or less overnight, although Gerry Williams recalls that boys of a certain age were not to be put off so easily. Forays were often made to gain access to the airfield, which was surprisingly easy, despite the warnings of the armed guards patrolling with dogs and access was achieved on a more or less daily basis. Assuming the guards carried out their duties diligently, it can only be surmised that the odd blind eye was turned!

Most operational stations enjoyed the regular rounds of the civilian Women's Royal Voluntary Service (WRVS) or the service Navy, Army, Air Force Institute (NAAFI) vans, bringing welcome cups of tea, slices of cake, sandwiches or buns (known, perhaps less politely, as 'rock-wads' in RAF slang), which enabled the men to take a well earned break. One former member of the NAAFI organisation, still living locally, is Mrs. Stevens (nee Stone), an undertaker's daughter from York.

Miss Stone was keen to join an organisation as the war progressed and she chose the NAAFI. Once her application was accepted, she was invited to Derby where she undertook a two day driving course, at the end of which she was taken to a line of vans and given a set of keys along with the words "*you're posted to Ashbourne, off you go!*" With this ringing in here ears, the young Miss Stone arrived at the town of Ashbourne and made her way onto the airfield via the main gate. Unfortunately, not knowing where she was and not being aware of the airfield layout, she soon found herself trundling down the main runway in her newly-issued NAAFI van! With the potential for aircraft to land at any time she had to be stopped and eventually a young airman was able to do just that and guide the errant NAAFI driver to her rightful place. Several other encounters and social events later and the two would become Mr and Mrs Stevens. They are happily married and live in the Ashbourne area today.

Mr and Mrs Stevens' wedding photograph.

(via Mr & Mrs Stevens' private collection)

The build-up continued apace during mid-1942 and the arrival of 81 OTU's Wellingtons was anticipated, which would enable crew training to begin. It was not to be. The earlier visit by Air Marshal Harris, which saw Ashbourne downgraded from an operational bomber airfield to a training airfield, impacted on Ashbourne once again. Bomber Command's 81 OTU was to leave Ashbourne and relocate to Whitchurch Heath airfield in

Shropshire with Sleap airfield (also in Shropshire) as the satellite station. The whole process which was undertaken to have 81 OTU up and running was now in reverse with men and equipment leaving Ashbourne for their new homes further south.

By the 1st September 1942, 81 OTU had left Ashbourne and all that remained of the RAF presence was a small working party who would act as caretakers, pending the arrival of the next unit. There now followed a very quiet period in Ashbourne's history; the once-perceived heavy bomber airfield, relegated to a training airfield was again relegated, this time to little more than a storage facility. Meanwhile, construction of the satellite airfield at Darley Moor was commencing steadily.

During this time, the whole Operational Training Unit structure was being reorganised and expanded. This saw 92 Group's area of responsibility move geographically to the south and 93 (Training) Group, Bomber Command, along with the other Group airfields of Lichfield and Hixon, both in Staffordshire and Wymesmold, in Leicestershire. would now assume responsibility for Ashbourne and Darley Moor from its Eggington Hall Headquarters near the River Dove, a short distance to the north of Ashbourne. Yet again, administrative changes would dictate that Ashbourne and latterly, Darley Moor, would never serve as bomber OTU stations as the airfield was next transferred from 93 Group Bomber Command to 70 Group Army Co-Operation Command. Finally, the unit that would be based at and become more or less synonymous with Ashbourne, would be 42 Operational Training Unit, then based at RAF Andover, Hampshire. The Commanding Officer after the transfer would be Sqn. Ldr. Peters and it was anticipated that 42 OTU would be fully established at Ashbourne by the end of October 1942.

On the 11th October 1942 Sqn. Ldr. Jordon, the Signals Officer for 42 OTU, arrived at Ashbourne, the establishment of signalling and communication being a priority. Four officers and sixty-four other ranks arrived from Andover on October the 15th. The Operations Record Book (ORB) for RAF Ashbourne records thirty-five officers and eighty-one other ranks arriving on October the19th. The same day, the aircraft which would be operationally based here finally began to land at Ashbourne. Mid-afternoon saw the arrival of a Westland Lysander over the airfield which attracted the attention of the local populace, who made their way to the airfield to watch the landings. The Lysander touched down and was followed in by the rest of the aircraft of 42 OTU which had made the journey from Andover. The Derby road was now lined with crowds of people who gathered to watch the safe arrival of the Blenheims, Whitleys, Ansons and Oxfords.

The following day, October 20th, saw the arrival of the initial WAAF contingent, comprising of nine officers and seventy-five other ranks. The 22nd of October saw a change in the Commanding Officer, Wing Commander Skelton taking control of RAF Ashbourne. The same day also saw another four officers and four other ranks arrive. At last, the airfield was becoming a very busy place. During the rest of October, men and equipment were arriving on a daily basis and things looked to be very much on course for 42 OTU to be operational by the end of that month as planned.

On the 29th of October, with over 700 personnel based at Ashbourne, Wing Commander Skelton relinquished command, to be taken over by Group Captain Hamilton. Along with Hamilton came his personal aircraft, a Messerschmitt Bf.108 Taifun[1], which caused a small stir amongst those personnel not expecting to see an impressed enemy aircraft.

At last, Ashbourne was an operational training airfield with aircraft based upon it; 42 OTU could now get on with their purpose – training.

---

1 Messerschmitt Bf108B-1 Taifun, RAF Serial AW167. Formerly D-IJHW. The aircraft was sold in September 1946 and became G-AFZO. Now de-registered.

Messerschmitt Bf108 Taifun, similar to the one belonging to Group Capitan Hamilton, although not in the Luftwaffe scheme!
(Stan Percy, 1979)

TRAINING BEGINS

Before the training regime is examined it is worth looking at the path which would bring air crew to their Operational Training Unit.

After volunteering for flying duties (it is worth remembering that all Royal Air Force air crew were volunteers), the would-be members would be summoned to attend an Air Crew Reception Centre (ACRC) for uniform issue, medicals and swimming tests. After elementary parading of the prospective air crew, the cadets were then posted to an Initial Training Wing (ITW).

The ITW's were largely situated at coastal holiday resorts as they had ample accommodation in the form of hotels and guest houses no longer being used by visitors. Blackpool, Aberystwyth, Newquay, Torquay, Brighton and Scarborough were among fifteen such locations. Here, the cadets, distinguished by a white flash to the front of their caps, went through a twelve week course of physical and theoretical training. The physical element consisted of gym work and cross country running while the theoretical aspects embraced navigation, astronomy, meteorology, theory of flight, armaments, map reading, signals, aircraft recognition, health and first aid. These courses were intensive and many would agree that at the end of their ITW period, they were probably at their peak of fitness and well indoctrinated in the ways of the Royal Air Force.

The next stage of training varied according to the category of air crew that the cadet had been selected for and also dictated the units to which they would be posted for the next phase: Pilot, Navigator and Bomb Aimer (PNBs), would find themselves at Elementary Flying Training Schools (EFTSs). Here, PNB cadets were given around twelve hours flying, usually in de Havilland dH.86 Tiger Moths.

Those who did well were likely to go on to become pilots, although this was never guaranteed as the operational demands of the Royal Air Force dictated a need for navigators or bomb aimers. This became noticeable as more four engined heavy aircraft (Short Stirlings, Handley Page Halifaxes and the Avro Lancaster), came into service with Bomber Command. These aircraft required two new crew members, a Flight Engineer, to replace the second pilot and an additional Air Gunner.

Crew members selected as Wireless Operators, Air Gunners and later, Flight Engineers, had their own specialised training schools. Very early in the war it was realised that the training of pilots, Navigators and Bomb Aimers in the British Isles was not wholly ideal. Poor weather often prevented flying, causing lengthy delays in training and also many accidents, particularly in regions of high ground. The skies over Britain were becoming more crowded, so the decision to relocate initial training was made, in co-operation with Canada, south Africa, southern Rhodesia, Kenya, Australia and New Zealand – to create the Empire Air Training Scheme (EATS). These countries already had their own training regimes in place but many of the airfields now found themselves hosting airmen from the UK. Many cadets were also posted to the United States.

At the conclusion of this excursion abroad, the cadets would have been training for eighteen months, sometimes longer, owing to hold-ups between courses and the usually lengthy sea voyages to and from the far-flung Dominions. Upon completion, the cadets would graduate; this 'passing out' marked a significant change in status for the successful airmen. First they received their brevet (an aircrew brevet is the badge worn on the left breast, above any medal ribbons, by qualified aircrew) in a ceremonial 'Wings Parade'. They were then automatically promoted to the rank of Sergeant or awarded a commission to Officer and the white flash (indicating 'air crew under training'), was removed from their caps. Also welcomed was the fact that they received an increase in pay! Upon return to the UK, there was usually a course at an Advanced Flying Unit (AFU) to acclimatise the crews with to realities of flying in Britain, the inherent dangers of rapidly changing weather conditions, the black-out, and the possibility of enemy intruder operations.

The direction of the courses was not rigidly adhered to; variations could and did occur. For example, Ken Rusby (who sadly would meet his fate in Albemarle V1610 at Boston, Lincolnshire. This incident will be discussed in detail later), had trained in Rhodesia, having sailed there on the 13th April 1942 aboard *Highland Princess*. Whilst there, he was posted to 12 Flight, Hillside ITW in May 1942. Having passed at ITW, his next posting was to 27 EFTS at Induna from October 1942.

The next move for Ken was on to 24 Bombing & Navigation School, based at Moffat, in December 1942, on Course No. 14X. Ken passed out in June 1943 and returned to the UK on 26th July 1943 aboard the *Mauretania*. After attending 2 (Observers) Advanced Flying Unit, he was posted to 42 OTU at Ashbourne in December 1943, where he joined Number 51 flying course. Ken was one of thousands of airmen to take a similar path.

The OTUs were a critical stage in the development of the crew as this was where all of the aircrew trades from their respective initial and later specialist courses came together. Up to this point, pilots had trained with pilots, navigators with navigators and so on.

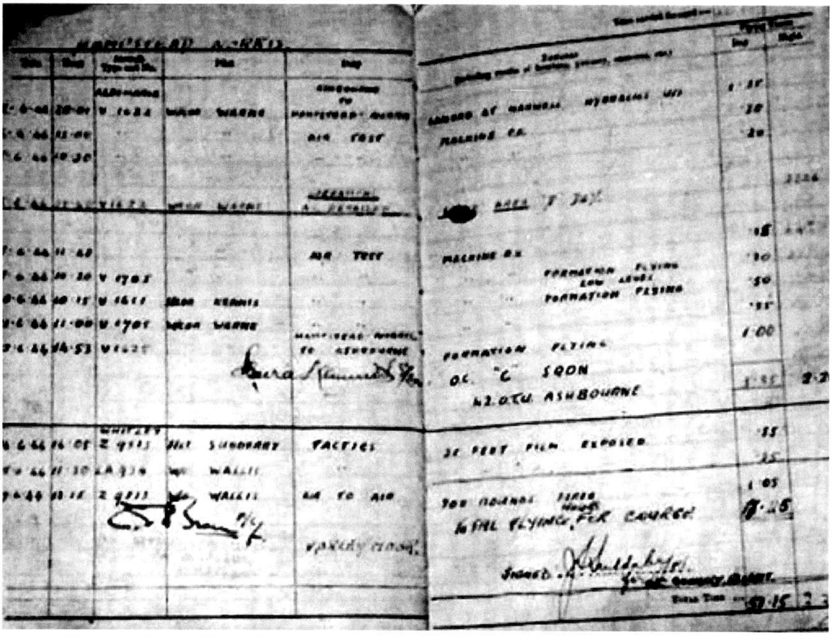

Pages from Ken Rusby's logbook relating to his transfer to RAF Ashbourne. (via Ken Rusby Jr.)

One of the first events upon arrival at OTU was the ritual of 'crewing up', where all personnel were assembled into one of the hangars to form their final teams. To many, it seemed a most haphazard method of forming what would become an operational crew. However, despite there being such a mixture of personalities, nationalities, ranks and social backgrounds, through flying together, depending on each other and the resulting respect for one another, strong bonds were formed. Years later, some of these ties are still very strong, as witnessed by the many Squadron and other unit Associations, along with long-lasting individual friendships.

Ken Rusby and crew socialising in Ashbourne. (via Ken Rusby Jnr.)

Part of the essential team-building exercise! Ken Rusby, beer glass in hand. (via Ken Rusby Jnr.)

Training was carried out in numbered courses, for example, number 38 Course, has a detailed reference in the Unit's ORB. Seven crews were received for training on Whitleys, who had already undergone an OTU course in Canada on Lockheed Venturas. Reporting for the course were twelve pilots, twelve Navigator/Bomb Aimers, twelve Wireless Operators/Air Gunners and seven Air Gunners. The courses consisted of flying and ground instruction in the and Link Trainer buildings. The Bombing Teacher/Turret Trainer building was a tall building, its purpose being to give crews a simulation of night flying and bomb aiming over enemy territory. The relevant crew-member s (Navigtors and Bomb Aimers) were housed at the top of the building with a representation of a target below them.

The Turret Trainer section housed a hemispherical metal frame, covered with laths and hessian and plastered over, painted flat white to form a vertical 180° parabolic screen. In front of the screen, on scaffolding, would have been an aircraft gun turret above which was a platform mounting a projector. With the doors closed and the room darkened, the projector would show the moving image of a target aircraft on the screen. The trainee gunner would have to track the target, apply deflection and 'open fire'. When he did, a spotlight, bore-sighted with the guns, would shine a yellow spot onto the screen showing the instructor where the gunner was aiming. The trainee gunner had to wear yellow tinted goggles so he could not see the spot.

The Link Trainer was an early form of flight simulator, intended to instruct pilots in the art of instrument-only flying, without leaving the ground. First devised towards the end of the 1920s by Edwin Link, the son of the owner of the Link Piano and Organ Company of New York, the Trainer was based on the technology in use at his father's factory. The Trainer, in which the pilot was totally enclosed, was mounted on a universal joint on a turntable thus permitting movement in roll, pitch, and yaw. Motion was provided by a system of vacuum operated bellows, which were controlled by valves attached to the pilot's controls. The basic instrument panel comprised many of the common flight attitude instruments in an aircraft: artificial horizon, turn and bank indicator, rate of climb indicator and so on, connected to the instructor's control desk.

Link Trainer. This particular example is a Type D2, constructed in 1942 by the Link Aviation Devices Company, New York. (Newark Air Museum, Nottinghamshire, Noel J. Ryan, 2006)

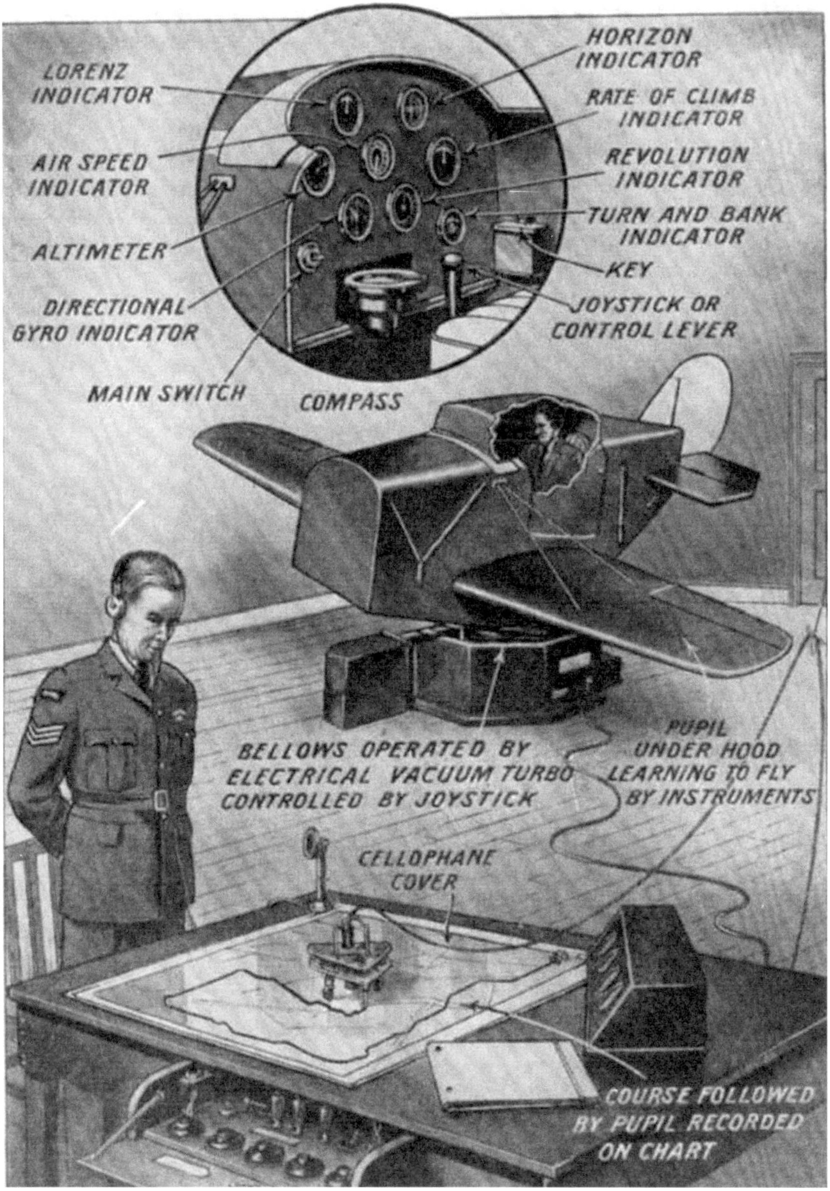

A contemporary instructional poster for the Link Trainer (via Cyberheritage.co.uk)

The instructor's desk was fitted with a flight recorder, or 'Crab', which was linked to the Trainer and 'driven' round the cellophane-surfaced desk, marking the course flown by the pilot in the cockpit. The instructor also had a set of repeated instruments, duplicating those in the cockpit of the Link Trainer itself, so the progress of the student could be monitored. Intercom facilities and controls for the navigation aids were also provided.

Link Trainer controller's desk. This example is at Newark Air Museum, Nottinghamshire. (Noel J. Ryan, 2006)

At times, security at the two airfields could, at best, be described as relaxed. A combination of this and the befriending of a NAAFI girl, as recounted by Mrs. Steven, saw at least one (unnamed) local schoolboy enjoy his first "flight" courtesy of a few hours on the Link Trainer at Ashbourne! Both Ashbourne and Darley Moor had large instructional sites with a variety of buildings. The largest at Ashbourne was the Gunnery and Crew Procedure building, a large area where a variety of tasks were practiced involving the entire crew in relation to their individual posts within the aircraft.

Instruction for preventing fire on crashing, an essential part of crew procedure. (via Cyberheritage.co.uk)

As well as learning the arts of navigation and gunnery, other vital instruction included aircraft evacuation and dinghy drill - very important given the vast areas of sea to be crossed during the operations. Where available, dinghy drill would have been carried out in a purpose-built dinghy pool on some airfields, although local swimming pools, ponds and lakes were often utilised. The latter was the case for 42 OTU - one of the lakes in Osmaston Park, in the grounds of Osmaston Hall, two miles to the south of Ashbourne airfield was one of the locations used for this purpose.

Training consisted of both day and night flying, although this was always subject to the local weather conditions. Close scrutiny of the Unit's ORB for April 1944 gives an example of how the courses could be affected:

> "*16th April 1944, weather cloudy no flying programme carried out*"
>
> "*17th April 1944, Cloudy. Day flying from 18.36 - 19.36, night flying cancelled*"
>
> "*18th April 1944, weather fine, hazy light winds. Day flying programme carried out from 11.00 - 20.17, night flying from 20.56 – 21.41*"

The conditions worsened as the 19th of April was recorded as "*Rain all day, no flying*". During this week it was not until the 20th when the courses could get back on track with the ORB recording the weather as "*... fine, good visibility moderate winds. Day flying carried out from 07.17 - 18.57 and night flying from 21.45 – 05.58*" As a matter of interest, a further two entries for the 20th April are recorded, the first of these being a "*... discussion group held in the station headquarters: Subject is, is the average WAAF better off financially in the service than in civilian life?*". This was possibly quite an interesting discussion and undoubtedly would have resulted in some very interesting remarks. Unfortunately, the outcome is not recorded in the ORB! The other entry for the 20th of April was noted by the Station Medical Officer in the ORB:

> "*... an outbreak on enteritis between Friday, 7th and Sunday 16th April. Twenty-one cases presented themselves for treatment.*"

The intervention of bad weather, whilst obviously disrupting the flying regime, would not see the trainees merely sitting around idle. The aforementioned ground training devices would see greater use, since as much training as possible would be condensed into the time available, thus maximising the use of the technical and training facilities.

In general, the flying training programme at an OTU consisted of day and night take offs and landings, known as 'circuits and bumps', cross country navigation flights often taking up to five hours ranging far over the Midlands, into Lincolnshire or Yorkshire and out over the Irish Sea and the mountains of Wales. Resupply missions were also practiced on the bombing ranges, the 'bombing' would consist of load dropping of either munitions, general supplies or medical supplies. As an Army Co-Operation training unit, close support tactical bombing was also undertaken by most of the twin-engined types at the Carsington Range. A reminder of the past use of the area still exists, in the form of one of the range quadrant towers, which is close to a car park along the western edge of the lake.

The remaining quadrant tower at Carsington Water, Derbyshire. (Tony Lack)

Another major airborne exercise was fighter affiliation, in which fighter aircraft, usually Hurricanes or Spitfires, made mock attacks on the bombers and transports. The pilot of the defending aircraft did his best to shake the fighter off, often employing the 'corkscrew manoeuvre' - a stomach-churning, twisting and turning evasive tactic which saw the target aircraft being violently thrown into dives, climbs and weaving manoeuvres. Live firing exercises entailed the use of a drogue, towed by one of the units Lysanders or Martinets, over the Kinder Scout Aerial Gunnery Range.

A Spitfire MK. IX during a fighter affiliation exercise - a familiar sight to the trainee gunners and pilots of Ashbourne and Darley Moor. (Tony Lack, 1945)

AIRBORNE OPERATIONS IN CONTEXT

Glider operations by the Luftwaffe's Air Assault divisions in support of the Wehrmacht in the opening stages of World War 2 had already shown the potential of the delivery of troops and equipment by air. Early German operations, which had served as a wake up call to the Allies, were the invasions of Belgium and later, Crete. The Luftwaffe, using one of the first successful assault gliders, the DFS230, began the Belgian airborne operations on May 10th, 1940. In the half-light of dawn, shortly after 5 am, ten DFS230s carrying a total of 78 assault troops arrived, having been released from their towing aircraft whilst still in German airspace. The landing took place virtually on top of a huge Belgian fort, Eben Emael, a barrier to Hitler's invasion of Belgium and Holland, not far from Maastericht.

Perhaps one of the most notable glider operations which influenced Allied operational thinking regarding gliders and assault was the airborne invasion of Crete on the 20th May, 1941. This was a massive combined airborne invasion by gliders, troop transports, supply drops and actual landings by Junkers Ju. 52s. Many of these early operations of World War Two by the

Luftwaffe can be attributed to General Kurt Student, who is largely recognised as being the architect of this method of structured, airborne warfare (although the Soviet Union were also working hard in this method of troop delivery during the inter-War period).

Glider development was already underway in Britain but it was becoming clear that the successful use of these aircraft types, in the undertaking of an assault on a specific target, could have a significant tactical effect. The Airspeed AS.51 Horsa was the largest of the Allied gliders to be utilised in the War years. It was not, however, the design which could be considered a cause for concern, rather its deployment. The first use of the aircraft was against the heavy water plant under Nazi control at Rjukan in Norway (the night of 19th/20th November, 1942 – *Operation Freshman*). This resulted in failure and many of the troops were eventually caught and executed on the direct orders of Hitler.

A rather more successful deployment of glider-delivered forces was the invasion of Sicily (*Operation Husky*, on the 9th/10th July, 1943). As with many airborne invasions up to this time, both Allied and Axis, the number of gliders used was small in relation to the overall number of troops deployed. The glider had begun to prove its worth in specialised, precise landings, where a concentration of troops was needed to secure a position quickly and by surprise.

During 1942-1943, glider and support operations were considered a viable means of tactical warfare and it fell to units such as 42 OTU amongst others, to refine the art. The training was intensive, usually involving around eighty hours flying time. As previously noted the weather, along with other factors, could delay a course for long periods. These experiences and others are described by Walter John Howes. He was at Ashbourne on 55 course in March 1944 and extracts from his letters home highlight the problems at the OTU.

Number 55 course at 42 OTU, Ashbourne. (via Kath Howes)

23/3/44 "Tomorrow morning we start off with a clothing parade and then the crews go off to the satellite (Darley Moor) and we settle down to a week on the link (Link trainer). One day I'll be on from 9-10 & 1.45 - 2.45, the next day will be from 10 - 11 & 2.45 - 3.45 and so on. Four weeks day flying and four weeks night flying"

16/4/44 "Absolutely no news, weather has been bad. AOC (Air Officer Commanding) did not turn up to interview us. We've been waiting around down at the flight line all day. I shall probably be night flying by the end of May"

19/4/44 " We were not called for early detail this morning and there has been no flying all day. I've just been sewing my service chevrons on my battle dress but I'm dashed if I'm going to sew them on my uniforms until I absolutely have to. They are awful things really and consist of painted calico. I haven't tried mine in the rain but I'm told the colour runs as soon as it gets wet. Someone worked out that this issue cost the country £40,000. How much better it would have been to use that money for a pay increase."

20/4/44 "For the latter part of May, if not for the whole month, I shall be on night flying, that means my being up here on the camp from 6pm to 7am every night. It was quite a shock to be woken at 4.30 this morning for flying. Almost miraculously the weather cleared, after breakfast in the airmen's mess I was down at the line by 5.30, supposedly for a 7am take off. Actually it was 7.30 before we got away and after a check circuit with the duty instructor I started a 3 hour detail of circuits and landings with my crew. I was certainly sore by the time we finished & was most annoyed to find myself only credited with 2 hours & 35 minutes. Times are kept by the people in the control tower & somehow they slipped up & must have missed our last landing, so we were swindled out of a hard earned half hour. Weather closed in and we flew no more. I'm afraid I don't understand how they organise this flight, Pegler, Brazier & Lacey all got about six hours flying today and though I'm way behind I only got three. Wade is still grounded and another man is having trouble and hasn't soloed yet. The CFI (Chief Flying Instructor) *said today that he wanted to give us plenty of flying so that we could get leave at the end of the month, sounds good!"*

23/4/44 " I flew yesterday afternoon from 4.15 - 7.30, an hour advanced dual & two hours solo and thus completely missed tea. Arriving at the mess five minutes after dinner we did not get a meal and after much scrounging managed to get some cold potatoes, lettuce, bread and cheese! The only people who get decently fed here are the admin staff who work from 9 -5 with two hours off for lunch. We with a working day from 4.30 am - 9.30 pm eat if and when we can"

26/4/44 "We are called, if the weather is fit, somewhere between 4.30 & 5 am & then have breakfast of some sort in the airmen's mess. Briefing is at 5.30 & takes about an hour to prepare everything for these trips. It takes another half an hour to get over to dispersal, sign for the aircraft and get it started up and taxied out to be airborne at 07.00"

1/5/44 "We took off yesterday for a complicated three and a half hour exercise but at 8.45 as we were approaching Peterborough we developed engine trouble. Peterborough was just a small grass field & with one engine dead and the other dying fast we finally squeezed in onto an American field further south. We got in quite safely & then had to wait for a plane from here to bring mechanics in & for the repairs to be completed. She was repaired temporarily & we staggered back here at 8.20 pm reaching the mess at 9 and bed at 10. I've got the flying bug worse than ever before & I just cannot get enough flying. A quick leave then at long last real operational flying. People really shooting at me and the best gunner in the air force shooting back......... At early breakfast I had a fried egg, back in our mess at 7.45 I had another one, then into town for tea I had a boiled egg!........ They decided to count the half trip we did on Saturday as a full cross country & that is the end of our day navigation. To finish day flying I just have to do three hours formation and two hours low level evasive action."

Walter John Howes qualified from 55 course 42 OTU at Ashbourne and went on to serve in 38 Group. Regrettably he lost his life towards the end of the war, aged just 22 years and 8 months.

Walter John Howes
(via Kath Howes)

Whilst training continued, great emphasis was placed on providing social facilities for the servicemen and women on the two airfields. Sports days were organised which would often include members of the local community. These, along with football and cricket matches, were held on the polo field in Ashbourne. In those days of rationing, advantage was taken of the post-event buffets, where "surplus" sausage rolls, sandwiches and buns would be secreted away by the ever present local boys. The opening of the station cinema (the *Astra*) on 26th April 1944 caused so much excitement that a lengthy entry was made in the ORB:

> *"Station cinema opened today. To mark the event a special presentation of "Life and Death of Colonel Blimp" was given (to be repeated tomorrow 27th April and Friday 28th April) at the invitation of PSI. Cinema equipment includes B.T.H. Sound reproducer system and twin Kales 12 units with automatic control of D.C. arcs. Sound and general presentation excellent. Training films are on demand and when received full use will be made of them for training of all ranks according to trades and subject matter of the films. It is proposed to run camp cinema for entertainment purposes on six nights of the week"*

The projection room extension to the Gymnasium and Chancel at Ashbourne – the Astra *cinema.*
(Noel J. Ryan, 2005)

As the war progressed and training intensified, the use of Darley Moor was made more formal. Previously, crews were transported to and from the satellite to carry out training, usually when Ashbourne became too crowded. This arrangement would change on the 3rd June 1944. Number 60 course, consisting of 19 Officers and 39 Sergeants, was attached to Darley Moor for fourteen days for navigation and gunnery training. This expedient was to continue, overcoming the difficulties in transporting crews to Darley Moor each day. It also eased complications over the distribution of rations.

D-DAY CONTRIBUTION

By early 1944, 38 Group consisted of nine operational Squadrons: four Squadrons equipped with the Armstrong Whitworth Albemarle of various Marks (295 Sqn coded '8E' and '8Z'; 296 Sqn coded '7C' and '9W'; 297 Sqn coded 'L5' and 'P5'; 570 Sqn coded 'V8'); one Squadron equipped with the Handley Page Halifax V (298 Sqn, 'A' Flight coded '8A' and 'B' Flight coded '8T') and four Squadrons equipped with the Short Stirling IV (299 Sqn coded '5G' and 'X9'; 190 Sqn coded 'G5' and 'L9'; 196 Sqn coded 'ZO' and '7T'; 620 Sqn coded 'D4' and 'QS'). On the 23rd February 1944, the Group was joined by 644 Sqn (Handley Page Halifax V, coded '9U'), formed from an echelon of 298 Sqn . This completed the Group's front-line Order of Battle in the run up to the invasion of mainland Europe, *Operation Overlord* – D-Day, June 6th, 1944.

Most of the crews from Ashbourne and Darley Moor, who had completed their courses, would find themselves posted to one of the front-line Albermarle Squadrons, whilst others were posted to units equipped with either the Stirling or the Halifax. The latter crews would now find themselves at a Heavy Conversion Unit (HCU) or Heavy Glider Conversion Unit (HGCU). Here, they would learn about the larger and heavier aircraft and the arts of dropping parachutists, aerial re-supply of ground troops and glider-towing. As the War progressed and the situation changed, the new crews were allocated to a front-line Squadron depending upon the operational requirements of the time. Whilst the successful completion of training courses was paramount, sometimes the demands of war would call for the premature use of these trainees. This was not a unique situation, as two years prior to *Overlord* just such a situation arose.

In February 1942 Bomber Command gained a new commander – Air Marshall Arthur T. Harris. Harris believed that at this time, Bomber Command was not being fully strategically utilized. He envisaged a massive raid comprising a thousand bombers attacking just one target; this would become famous as the *Thousand Plan*, the intention being that every German city would be attacked in this way forcing a surrender. In May 1942 however, Bomber Command comprised of just 37 front line Squadrons with only 17 of these being equipped with four engine heavy bombers, giving Harris about 400 serviceable aircraft, well below his target figure of 1000. Even with a suspension of operations for 48 hours prior to the raid to enable unserviceable aircraft to be made ready, a figure of around 500 was attainable. With the proposed inclusion of Coastal Command's aircraft and the addition of obsolete bombers the 1000 mark was just achievable. Coastal Command, however, refused to allow its aircraft to participate and the figure fell to 800. Harris, if he was to achieve his aim, had no choice but to call on Bomber Command's training units and aircraft. On May 30th 1942, over 1000 bomber aircraft attacked Cologne causing massive damage. At this time in the War, the actual logistics of such a task would mean that raids of this nature were the exception and not the rule; it would be much later before Bomber Command reached its full potency.

With the build up to *Overlord*, the front-line Squadrons of 38 Group (in a situation not dissimilar to the early 1000 Bomber raids), found their numbers swelled by aircraft sourced from the training units, including 42 OTU. However, this temporary reallocation of aircraft was by no means on the same scale as the 1000 bomber raids. In 1944 RAF Harwell in Oxfordshire came to be one of the most important airfields in 38 Group. It would be from here that on the night/morning of 5th/6th June 1944, the paratroopers of the 22nd Independent Parachute Company Pathfinders would take off in 6 Albemarles to be dropped behind enemy lines around the French City of Caen. The first Albemarle took off at 23.03 and carried Air Vice Marshall Leslie N. Hollinghurst, the Air Officer Commanding 38 Group. Their task was to mark the drop zone for the following glider and parachute wave, which would secure the vital bridges over the River Orne and the Caen Canal, to prevent a German counter-attack on the flank of the invading forces as D-Day progressed. One of these bridges would later become famous as *Pegasus Bridge*.

One of the satellite airfields of RAF Harwell was RAF Hampstead Norris, Berkshire and it was to here that the selected Albemarles and crews from Ashbourne and Darley Moor were sent. On the 2nd June, "C" Flight, 42 OTU, was moved on "temporary" duty to RAF Hampstead Norris. Thirty-two airmen of the Repair and Servicing Section, with Warrant Officer Juffs in charge were despatched, along with a further 28 Officers and 38 NCOs Leaving at 18:30 aboard Albermarles, they made the journey to the Berkshire airfield.

It is interesting to note that the ORB for RAF Hampstead Norris records a slightly different version in terms of numbers of personnel:

"*2.6.44 during the afternoon W/Cmdr Warne D.F.C. arrived from Ashbourne with a party consisting of 29 Officers, 27 Sergeants, and 31 ground crews*"

One of the crews to arrive at Hampstead Norris was that of Flt. Lt. J. A. Finn.

Table 5: Flt. Lt. Finn's crew.

Flt. Lt.	J. A. Finn	Pilot
Flt. Lt.	P. C. Morgan	Navigator/Bomber
F/O	D. F. Smart	Navigator/Bomber
P/O	G. R. Wellsman	Navigator/Bomber
F/O	A. L. Andrews	Wireless Operator/Air Gunner
Flt. Sgt.	R. Dunk	Wireless Operator/Air Gunner
Sgt	W. T. Francis	Air Gunner

The duplication of 'trades' within the crew positions reflects the fact that they were volunteers for this mission, a hastily assembled “scratch” crew. Their aircraft was Albemarle G.T. 1, serial number P1442. The pilot, Flt. Lt. Finn, was a staff pilot at Ashbourne and very experienced. Equally experienced was Flt. Lt. Percy Cyril Morgan, who had joined the Royal Air Force Volunteer Reserve (RAFVR) in 1939.

Flt. Sgt. (later Flt. Lt.) Percy Cyril Morgan D.F.M., Navigator/Bomber of Finn's crew in Albermarle P1442. (via Len Simm)

When war was declared, he was immediately called-up into the regular service and survived two complete tours of duty on bombing raids over France and Germany. During August 1941, he may have shot down two enemy night fighters in one night and it was for this action he was awarded his Distinguished Flying Medal (DFM). Had Morgan been a Commissioned Officer, he would have been awarded the Distinguished Flying Cross (DFC) - as the cutting sates. At the time, Morgan was a NCO and was a Sgt. Air Gunner with 58 Squadron flying Armstrong Whitworth Whitley aircraft from RAF Linton-on-Ouse, Yorkshire, as part of 4 Group Bomber Command.

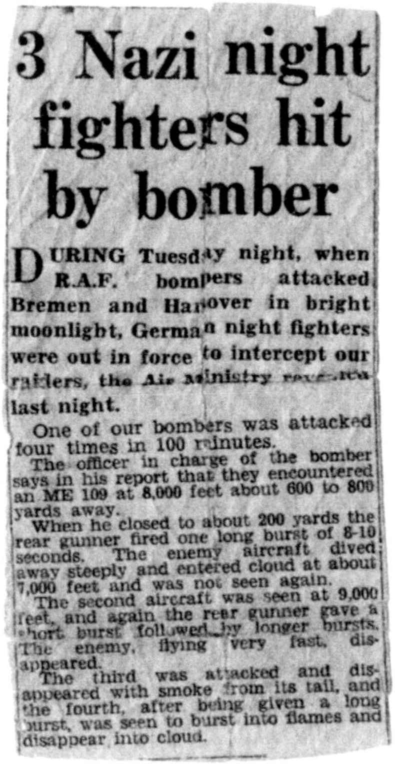

3 Nazi night fighters hit by bomber

DURING Tuesday night, when R.A.F. bombers attacked Bremen and Hanover in bright moonlight, German night fighters were out in force to intercept our raiders, the Air Ministry revealed last night.

One of our bombers was attacked four times in 100 minutes.

The officer in charge of the bomber says in his report that they encountered an ME 109 at 8,000 feet about 600 to 800 yards away.

When he closed to about 200 yards the rear gunner fired one long burst of 8-10 seconds. The enemy aircraft dived away steeply and entered cloud at about 7,000 feet and was not seen again.

The second aircraft was seen at 9,000 feet, and again the rear gunner gave a short burst followed by longer bursts. The enemy, flying very fast, disappeared.

The third was attacked and disappeared with smoke from its tail, and the fourth, after being given a long burst, was seen to burst into flames and disappear into cloud.

Press cutting, regularly carried by Morgan, describing the action in which he downed two of the aircraft that attacked the bomber in which he was flying.

This cutting survived Morgan's loss due to the fact that at the time he was killed, all aircrew were required to fly 'sterile' – having no items other than those officially endorsed for identification purposes.

(via Len Simm)

After the completion of his second tour of operations he was promoted to Flight Lieutenant and specialised in navigation. After a variety of postings and transfers, he was eventually based at Ashbourne as a Navigator Instructor. Both Finn (the Pilot) and Morgan had only a few days to settle in at Hampstead Norris after the call came for *Overlord* crews to be mustered from Ashbourne and Darley Moor. Circumstances meant events were moving quickly now, and although the actual day of the operation they would undertake was yet to be disclosed to those taking part (the date had already been chosen (5th June, 1944), due to bad weather in and over the English Channel, was postponed by twenty-four hours to the 6th June), the crew knew something would happen soon. An air of anticipation descended on the airfield.

On the 3rd June the normal flying programme was discontinued and on the following day, Hampstead Norris' ORB notes that "*There has been very little activity today".* The entry for the following day suggests that the moment was upon them, as it was recorded that the "*...operational aircraft were air tested during the day and marshalled in readiness for the night take off.*"

On the night of the 5th June 1944, a massive air armada consisting of aircraft from all Commands; Coastal, Bomber and Fighter, as well as the Allied Expeditionary Air Force Command, which contained elements of 38 Group, was either heading to the Continent or conducting operations over the English Channel. The Allied Expeditionary Force consisted in total of 1287 aircraft of which 1140 (873 American C-47 Skytrains of various Troop Carrier Groups, 129 RAF Dakotas, 47 Albemarles and 91 Stirlings), were on parachute dropping operations. The other 147 aircraft (comprising 52 American C-47 Skytrains, 13 RAF Dakotas, 45 Albemarles and 37 Halifaxes), were engaged on glider towing duties. Of these aircraft 25 failed to return to base, comprising 16 C-47s, 5 Stirlings, 2 RAF Dakotas, 1 Halifax and 1 Albemarle - P1442 from 42 OTU.

The last flight of Albemarle P1442 began on the Hampstead Norris runway late in the evening of the 5th June. Nine Albemarles, including the four drawn from Ashbourne, were scheduled to take part, although one (*V-Victor*) suffered engine trouble and was unable to take part. The first of the three remaining 42 OTU Albemarles took off at 23.00, followed at short intervals by the other aircraft, P1442 becoming airborne at 23.48.

The task of P1442 was, according to airman Flt. Lt. Leslie A. Mayhew (who also took part in the same operation)

> "*...to upset the enemy's radio location system* [radar] *and to fool him into believing that the main airborne landings were taking place at a point many miles from the points chosen for that force...*". He goes on to further comment that the mission was successful as "*The Huns announced landings in the area over which we had flown.*" (extracted from correspondence by Flt. Lt. Mayhew to Morgan's wife on the 30th June 1944).

The actual method of confusing the German radar involved bundles of thin strips of aluminium codenamed *Window*. The type of *Window* used for the *Overlord* operation was primarily 'Type MB' (there were twelve types in all), which was designed to counter-measure the German ground radar types *Freya* and FuG220, also the FuG216, 217 and 218, covering the frequency range of 70 to 200 MHz. Each bundle of strips of Type MB, which measured 70.8 inches (180cm) by 2 inches (5 cm), was dropped at timed intervals, two bundles at a time. The effect on the German radar was to present a false picture of a 'spoof' air raid.

The lost Armstrong Whitworth Albemarle, P1442 of 42 OTU (via Len Simm)

Research undertaken by Len Simm, a family relative, has shed some light onto what happened to Albemarle P1442, although the final fate of this aircraft was never been fully established, as no wreckage was ever found and subsequently, no bodies recovered. There were many RAF and other Allied aircraft shot down on D-Day and the days following. Many met their fate in the shallow valley that stretches between Falaise and the southern approaches to Caen. These aircraft would have fallen at great speed. On impact, they usually buried themselves many feet underground leaving only a crater and the odd piece of wreckage scattered as surface debris. In northern France during June 1944, whilst the local farmers were beginning to gather in the early harvest, they witnessed many air crashes. When a plane crashed onto arable land the farmer, despite his grief and sorrow regarding the plane and its crew, could not afford the time or labour to extract the wreck from deep underground. Having a living to make, they would simply fill in the crater and sow new seed over the wreck. Unless P1442 was lost over the English Channel, it can only be speculated that it may have been entombed in such a way. During the night and early morning of the 5th/6th June there was a tremendous concentration of shipping in the English Channel and a number of special Air Sea Rescue missions were also being flown therefore, if lost over the Channel, the odds of the crew being picked up, or at least of finding some wreckage of P1442, would have been high.

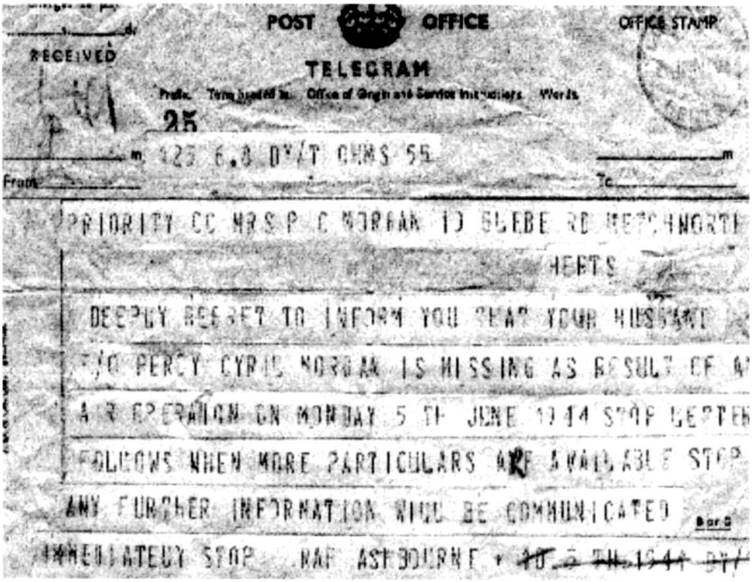
POST OFFICE

TELEGRAM

OFFICE STAMP

RECEIVED

25

PRIORITY CC MRS P C MORGAN 13 GLEBE RD LETCHWORTH
HERTS

DEEPLY REGRET TO INFORM YOU THAT YOUR HUSBAND
F/O PERCY CYRIL MORGAN IS MISSING AS RESULT OF AN
AIR OPERATION ON MONDAY 5 TH JUNE 1944 STOP LETTER
FOLLOWS WHEN MORE PARTICULARS ARE AVAILABLE STOP
ANY FURTHER INFORMATION WILL BE COMMUNICATED
IMMEDIATELY STOP RAF ASHBOURNE

The telegram from the station Commanding Officer at Ashbourne following P1442s failure to return from the operations of D-Day.
(via Len Simm)

"DEEPLY REGRET TO INFORM YOU THAT YOUR HUSBAND F/O PERCY CYRIL MORGAN IS MISSING AS A RESULT OF AN AIR OPERATION ON MONDAY 5 TH JUNE 1944. LETTER FOLLOWS WHEN MORE PARTICULARS ARE AVAILABLE. ANY FURTHER INFORMATION WILL BE COMMUNICATED IMMEADIATLY. RAF ASHBOURNE

(via Len Simm)

On the 5th September 1944 Mrs Morgan received a letter from the Air Ministry which confirmed that Percy Cyril Morgan and his Albermarle crew were, indeed, lost.

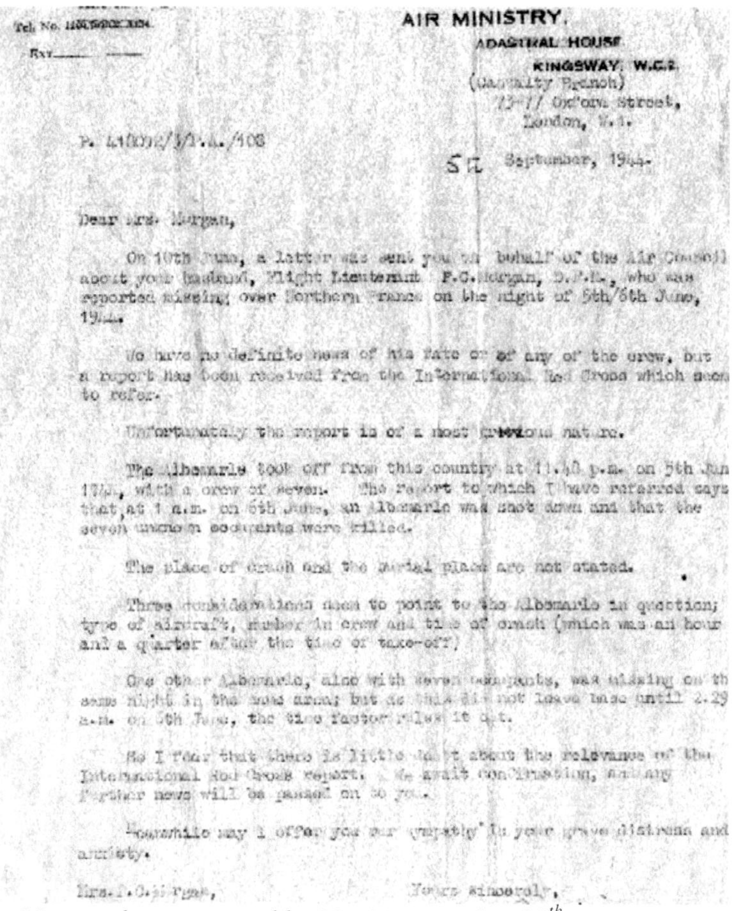

Tel. No. [illegible]

Ext. ______

AIR MINISTRY.

ADASTRAL HOUSE

KINGSWAY, W.C.2.

(Casualty Branch)

73-77 Oxford Street,

London, W.1.

P. [illegible]/P.4.A./408

5th September, 1944.

Dear Mrs. Morgan,

On 10th June, a letter was sent you on behalf of the Air Council about your husband, Flight Lieutenant P.C. Morgan, D.F.M., who was reported missing over Northern France on the night of 5th/6th June, 1944.

We have no definite news of his fate or of any of the crew, but a report has been received from the International Red Cross which seems to refer.

Unfortunately the report is of a most grievous nature.

The Albemarle took off from this country at 11.40 p.m. on 5th June 1944, with a crew of seven. The report to which I have referred says that at 1 a.m. on 6th June, an Albemarle was shot down and that the seven unknown occupants were killed.

The place of crash and the burial place are not stated.

Three considerations seem to point to the Albemarle in question; type of aircraft, number in crew and time of crash (which was an hour and a quarter after the time of take-off).

One other Albemarle, also with seven occupants, was missing on the same night in the same area; but as this did not leave base until 2.29 a.m. on 6th June, the time factor rules it out.

So I fear that there is little doubt about the relevance of the International Red Cross report. We await confirmation, and any further news will be passed on to you.

Meanwhile may I offer you our sympathy in your grave distress and anxiety.

Mrs. P.C. Morgan,

Yours sincerely,

Air Ministry letter received by Mrs Morgan, dated 5th September, 1944 (via Len Simm)

Air Ministry
Adastral House
Kingsway, WC2
(Casualty Branch)
73-77 Oxford Street
London W1
5th September 1944

Dear Mrs Morgan

On 10th June, a letter was sent to you on behalf of the Air Council about your husband, Flight Lieutenant P.C. Morgan, DFM., who was reported missing over northern France on the night of 5th/6th June, 1944.

We have no definite news of his fate or of any of the crew, but a report has been received from the International Red Cross.

Unfortunately the report is of a most grievous nature.

The Albemarle took off from this country at 11.48 p.m. on 5th June 1944, with a crew of seven. The report to which I have referred says that, at 1 a.m. on 6th June, an Albemarle was shot down and that the seven unknown occupants were killed.

The place of the crash and the burial place are not stated.

Three considerations seem to point to the Albemarle in question; type of aircraft, number in crew and time of crash (which was an hour and a quarter after the time of take-off)

One other Albemarle, also with seven occupants, was missing on the same night in the same area; but as this did not leave base until 2.29 a.m. on 6th june, the time factor rules it out.

So I fear that there is little doubt about the relevance of the International Red Cross report. We await further confirmation, and any further news will be passed on to you. Meanwhile may I offer you our sympathy in your grave distress and anxiety."

D.F.C. KILLED

Crashed On Raid Over France

AWARDED the Distinguished Flying Cross in 1942 and veteran of 29 operational flights over enemy territory, Flying Officer P. Cyril Morgan, of Burgoyne-road, South Norwood, second son of Mrs. Marie Morgan and the late Mr. P. O. Morgan, has been killed on active service.

His 'plane, in which he was serving as a navigator, failed to return from a raid over Northern France on the night of June 5th-6th. The wreck of the aircraft, together with the seven bodies of its crew, has since been located in France.

A KEEN ATHLETE

Pilot Officer Morgan, who was 30, lived practically all his life in South Norwood, where he was educated at the Stanley Technical School and the South Norwood School, Birchanger-road. A keen athlete, he was a fine swimmer and a member of the Woodside Swimming Club.

He was also a member of the Beaconside Sports Club, of which he was a founder-member, and played in the Thornton Heath and District Football League.

Joining the R.A.F.V.R. in June, 1939, he enlisted for training at the beginning of the war, receiving his commission in 1943. He leaves a widow and two children, Roger, aged 2½, and Sheila, aged ten months.

BROTHER MISSING

His eldest brother, Sergeant Stanley Morgan, R.E.M.E., is serving in India. A younger brother, Sergeant Observer Wilfred Morgan, was reported missing after his aircraft failed to return from a raid on Essen in June, 1942.

Press cutting announcing Morgan's loss. (via Len Simm)

Ashbourne, Darley Moor and 42 OTU played a small but important part in what would be the turning point of the war in Europe. The final words on this episode are left to the ORB for 42 OTU, which reports:

> *"6-6-44: News that invasion of the continent had this day commenced received with deep sense of satisfaction by all ranks. Action taken immediately to check security measures. Aerodrome guards doubled as anti-sabotage measure. Four Albemarles from this station took part in this operation, based at Hampstead Norris. One aircraft reported missing with crew."*

Once the invasion of Europe was underway, Ashbourne and Darley Moor graduates could be found in many of the major air assault operations during the closing stages of the War. However, once victory in Europe was assured, the unit began to wind down. By the later part of 1943, many of the unit's aircraft were factory fresh, most notably the Whitleys and latterly, the Albermarles but by 1947, most of these aircraft had been struck from RAF charge and subsequently scrapped.

This was in the future still and for the rest of the war, the training schedule itself continued but claimed many victims from the stations, both as a result of mechanical failure or weather-related. The principal difference between these and the circumstances surrounding the disappearance of P1442 is that there had been closure. The crews and their aircrafts' location is known. However, subsequent searches by relatives of those missing aboard P1442, both in the UK and abroad have proven to be exhausting, frustrating and on occasions, fruitless but they carry on their search. This Chapter has been dedicated to the crew of P1442 and the efforts of Len Simm and his family.

5

ACCIDENTS & INCIDENTS

Like many stations housing training units, both would see their share of tragedy through the loss of aircraft and crews in flying accidents. Whilst it is a fact that the weather and geography were contributory to many accidents, there was a variety of other causes. The following examines some of these, giving an insight into the difficulties faced by the instructors and trainees alike and the sometimes confused nature of an incident and its subsequent investigation and recovery in more recent years

What becomes apparent in most cases was the needless loss of life and materials. The demands of the period during World War 2 for 'qualified' crews to equip the ever-expanding numbers of front-line operational squadrons, there was the need to 'get the job done'.

The first aircraft casualty at Ashbourne was not a 42 OTU aircraft but one from another RAF unit, 12 Squadron, RAF Binbrook, Lincolnshire. This incident occurred before the airfield was declared operational. On 6th January 1942, Vickers Wellington Mk. II W5514 coded PH-S, was one of a number of aircraft taking part in a raid on the French port of Brest. The aircraft was forced to take evasive action over the target area, resulting in Flt. Sgt. H. D. Bryant bailing out of the aircraft after receiving the order from the Captain, Pilot Officer (P/O) J. M. Garlick. It is not known to what extent the Wellington was damaged, or why the order to bale out was rescinded but the pilot managed to get the aircraft back to England.

The aircraft was unable to return to Binbrook, so the remainder of the crew (minus Bryant), were forced to look for an alternative airfield. Hunting around the north and Midlands, they eventually came across Ashbourne and made the decision to land. Unknown to the crew, the airfield was still under construction. At 23.48 hours, as it made its landing approach, the Wellington hit overhead power lines then collided with a lorry, before finally crash-landing on the partially finished runway. Fortunately the aircraft came to a halt with all on board surviving but much shaken.

Wellington Mk.IIs, similar to W5514, which crashed onto the unfinished runway at RAF Ashbourne. (The Brooklands Collection)

By October of 1942 flying training had at last started. The increased activity was to witness a steady catalogue of accidents and incidents being recorded in the stations ORB. All these accidents were investigated and the details recorded on Form 1180, the standard RAF Accident Record Form.

For example on the 7th November 1942, Bristol Blenheim Mk. IV N3567, took off from Ashbourne on a training flight. Shortly after, the aircraft stalled and crashed into trees one mile west of the airfield. On January 15th, 1943 another Blenheim Mk. IV, V5752, stalled in cloud and dived straight into the ground one mile south of Ashbourne airfield. At the same time, Darley Moor also began to accrue its own list of casualties - Blenheim Mk. I, L1234 on 28th March, 1943 and Whitley Mk. V Z9189 (27th July, 1943), both crashing on take-off.

In the early hours of April 7th 1943, Bristol Blenheim Mk IV V6078, took off from Ashbourne. The crew comprised P/O John Barry Welton (pilot), Eric Desmond Murphy (wireless operator) and Leslie Harold Redford (Navigator/Bomb Aimer). The purpose of the training flight was a navigation and wireless procedures exercise. The aircraft struck some trees shortly after take-off and crashed into a field near Matlock, Derbyshire.

Crash site of Bristol Blenheim Mk. IV V6078 near Matlock.

(Alan L. Clark, Peak District Air Accident Research.)

Whilst undercarriage collapses were not uncommon, Blenheim Mk. IV BA756 suffered from an unusual malady whilst landing at Ashbourne on the 25th April 1943. The controls had not been correctly assembled, resulting in the undercarriage being retracted on landing. The aircraft was written off by the ensuing fire.

Nearly three months later on the 9th July 1943, another Bristol Blenheim, this time Mk. V, AZ876, was lost on a local training sortie. The crew of the aircraft, F/O Michael Matthew (pilot), F/O Robert Andrew Whitmore (navigator/bomb aimer) and Sgt. Frederick Harry Doe (wireless operator/air gunner), took off from Ashbourne during the early hours of the morning. They were bound for the Carsington bombing range for an exercise. Shortly after take off, whilst flying between 2000 and 5000 feet, the aircraft dived into the ground near Belper in Derbyshire, killing all on board. The cause of the crash was never established. It was to be this incident which signalled the end of the Blenheims' career with 42 OTU. The Commanding Officer, Group Captain Hamilton, suspended training on the type a few days later and it was never to be used by 42 OTU again, being retired from the line.

The crash scene of Bristol Blenheim MK V AZ876 at Belper, Derbyshire in 2004. Note the slight depression in the ground and the stunted grass-growth at the point of impact.

(Alan L. Clark, Peak District Air Accident Research)

On the 4th August, 1943, a strange incident befell Armstrong Whitworth Whitley Mk. V serial N1505. Whilst on a night navigation exercise from Ashbourne, searchlight batteries on the west Coast illuminated the aircraft, apparently causing the pilot to become disorientated. Control of the aircraft was lost and it crashed into the sea with the loss of all on board. There were also other instances of Whitleys coming to grief whilst on navigational exercises, another example being on the 23rd August 1943. For reasons not established by the RAF accident board, Whitley Mk. V, serial T4339, crashed into the river Severn.

Escape axe from a Whitley aircraft, found near Ashbourne. These axes were provided for air crew to chop their way out of the aircraft after crashing or ditching. (Noel J Ryan. Axe courtesy of Gerry Williams)

Early September 1943 saw the arrival of the Armstrong Whitworth Albemarles at Ashbourne and Darley Moor as 42 OTU began to supplement its existing fleet of aircraft. To begin with, the build up of this type was in limited numbers and it would be some time before an Albemarle became a casualty.

The first of the type to be lost occurred on March 12th 1944. Albemarle S.T. Mk. II V1604 crashed at Bradley Lodge, close to Ashbourne whilst engaged on a cross-country navigational exercise. The crash killed the pilot, F/O J. D. M. Baille and the other four crew members whose names are not recorded. The RAF Accident Record Form 1180 notes that the aircraft had called for *Darky*. The *Darky* system was in place for an aircraft in distress (either lost or with other problems), to call up and request a homing to the nearest airfield. By taking bearings both by radio and telephone, the latter being undertaken by the Royal Observer Corps, a plot and consequently a homing bearing could be given to the crew. The Form 1180 relating to this incident notes the pilot's flying hours; 236 with 41 hours on the Albemarle and of these, his night flying hours were a total of 56 with 7 hours on the Albemarle. The Squadron Engineering Officer also makes a reference on the Form to the effect that there was "*...no sign of engine trouble...*". This was a brand new aircraft, being from a production batch from Armstrong Whitworth's sub-contractor, A.W. Hawksley's. It was an experienced pilot in an aircraft with a relatively short and known history. The actual cause was unknown.

A few days later on the 30th March 1944, Albemarle G. T. Mk. I, P1463 took off for a routine training flight, again from Ashbourne. Almost immediately the aircraft struck high-tension cables on Haven Hill and crashed at Bradbourne, about four miles north of Ashbourne. The crew, P/O Douglas Revitt, F/O Matthew Montague O'Connor, Flt. Sgt. Samuel Morrison and Sgt. Kenneth Scammell were all were killed in the incident. Research by Alan Clark of the Peak District Air Accident Research Group reveals that the first three crew members are all listed as pilots, with Sgt. Scammell being the Wireless Operator/Air Gunner. Further research by Mr. Clark (and backed up by the Commonwealth War Graves Commission), notes that all crew members, with the exception of F/O O'Connor, were from 55 Squadron which at this time was in Italy. Quite what they were doing in an Albemarle in Derbyshire is unclear.

Crash site of Albemarle P1463 at Bradbourne, Derbyshire. (Alan L. Clark, Peak District Air Accident Research.)

April 1944 saw no let up in the accidents involving the Albemarles. On the 15th of that month V1609, an S. T. Mk. II, out on a training sortie executed a low level turn near Hartford in Cheshire; the aircraft hit a chimney and crashed nearby. Eight days later its sister aircraft V1610 (also an S. T. Mk. II) was lost near Boston, Lincolnshire. In 1986, the incident was researched by the Lincolnshire Aircraft Recovery Group (LARG), based at east Kirkby Airfield. The LARG subsequently carried out a dig at the crash location. The following narrative, supplied by Dave Stubley of the LARG, details events surrounding the crash and subsequent recovery of some the aircraft's components.

THE LOSS AND RECOVERY OF ALBEMARLE S. T. MK. II V1610

The following account illustrates some of the confusion which often surrounded a Wartime incident and the subsequent frustrations faced by a dedicated team of volunteer aviation archaeologists.

"At just before quarter to three in the morning (02.43 hours) on the 23rd April 1944, the Albemarle took off for a routine low-level, cross country exercise at 2,500 feet. The aircraft left Ashbourne and headed east towards Sleaford, Lincolnshire. It had then turned back towards Newark, Nottinghamshire and then turned north to Malton in north Yorkshire. All seemed to be going well when it reached Malton and so following the next part of the exercise it turned south to head for Spalding back in Lincolnshire. Whilst over-flying Lincolnshire (near to RAF Coningsby), one hour twenty minutes into the exercise, the aircraft was suddenly shaken by a violent explosion and a fire in the port wing ensued. The pilot, Sgt. J. E. Hutchinson, gave the order to bale out as the aircraft started to lose height.

The Albemarle hit the ground at Kirton Fen, approx 4 miles from Coningsby and slid across a field near Gill Bridge Farm. At the end of the field it hit a large hedge and 'rabbit hill' where it exploded killing Sgt. Hutchinson, Sgt. K. Rusby and Sgt. A. A. Whittome. The other two members of the crew, Sgt's J. Davies and R. W. Thurgood, managed to bale out and survived.

Ken Rusby Snr. (via Ken Rusby Jnr)

Some doubt has arisen as to what happened on the night, reports have said that it was shot down by a German night fighter, as they were very active over east Anglia. However, local people feel certain that it was shot down by 'friendly fire' possibly from a Beaufighter that was based RAF Coleby Grange, Lincolnshire. A Court of Inquiry was held a few days later by the RAF into the incident of 23rd April, but the results are not known despite extensive research and may never be known. It is certain there was much confusion on the night because of the high number of German night fighters reaping much damage to returning aircraft from a raid on the marshalling yards at Hamm.

The LARG had known of the Albemarle crash for many years but it was not until 1986 that the site was accurately located and even then it could not be proven it was an Albemarle. After extensive research from the records available there were only a few Albemarle's listed as crashing in Lincolnshire and none fitted the criteria. Local reports again varied and even a date could not be ascertained. The Ministry of Defence would not issue a license to LARG without more information than just 'an Albemarle aircraft'.

Using Simon Parry's excellent book "Intruders over Britain" *there was even mention of an Albemarle V1610 which was shot down over Great Yarmouth, over 100 miles away so this was discounted, the group where in a 'quandary'. We had missed the 'recovery envelope time' and so the farmer re-cropped his land and we would have to wait for another year. With reports of a Blenheim also crashing in the area whilst landing at RAF Coningsby we thought this must be the case and it probably wasn't an Albemarle? Permission was duly sort for Blenheim L6744, the afore mentioned aircraft, and we were granted a license.*

Late summer 1988, recovery commenced using metal detectors and spades, the idea being that we could clear the top wreckage before a mechanical digger could lift out any deeper wreckage. Fairly close to the surface we found a propeller blade descending into the ground at 45 , hope of an engine being at the end was soon dispelled when it ended in a corroded 'stub'. Attention was soon drawn to a cylinder being unearthed at only 2 feet down, surrounded with pipes and wires we thought it could be part of the undercarriage. After much frantic digging it came out as a cylinder some 30 inches long and 8 inches in diameter, with no visible pipes or attachments. We were fairly certain it was not a bomb, but being mindful of photoflashes etc which could be as equally lethal, a decision was made to contact the EOD for their expert opinion of it.

A team of REMEs (Royal Electrical and Mechanical Engineers) *came up from Chatham, Kent despite them passing the main RAF EOD team at RAF Wittering just over the Lincs border in Cambs. Arriving later in the evening and not being able to identify the cylinder a controlled explosion was called for to look inside the item, but as the site was in a bone-dry former cornfield they requested that the Fire Brigade attended. At 11.00 in the evening, amidst many blue-flashing lights, the charge was detonated with a large flash. On examination it was found that the cylinder contained an un-identified liquid and the site was declared safe!*

The following weekend, with the attendance of the digger, the recovery turned out to be a bit of an anticlimax with no engine being found. Items recovered showed extensive signs of fire damage and included several shattered engine cylinders and parts. But no positive proof of identity. The only major item recovered in good condition was a propeller boss at a depth of seven feet. Though the engine cylinder parts were obviously not from a Blenheim the prop boss either, our hopes were again encouraged when a local chap turned up at the site and again insisted it was an Albemarle, but he also recalled that it was from a Derbyshire airfield and one of the crew was called Tony Whittome. This now tied in with a name listed in "Intruders over Britain" *as one of the crew of Albemarle V1610 of 42 O.T.U. from RAF Ashbourne. This now left the group with the problem of having recovered the wrong aircraft mentioned on the license. Contact was made with the MoD and the situation explained and much understanding was shown and the problem soon cleared up.*

Although the recovery was a little disappointing in what was found the group learned many lessons from the work, not least that however much research and paperwork is gone into, nothing can substitute the local knowledge around at the time.

Following the recovery, Ian McLachlan, author of "Night of the Intruders" *which chronicles the events of the disastrous night of the 22nd April 1944 when many American aircraft fell foul of the German night fighter intruders, offered to contact any surviving relatives of the crew of Albemarle V1610 as it also was part of the remit of his book. By sheer good luck he made contact with Ken Rusby, son of Sgt K. Rusby who was killed in V1610, Ken jnr had been researching his father's life but did not know that parts of the aircraft had been recovered. From this the LARG worked with Ken and his family and now there is a permanent dedicated memorial to the crew on display with the wreckage of V1610 at the Lincolnshire Aviation Heritage Centre, East Kirkby unveiled by Ken and his mother in 1992."*

Parts recovered from the crash site of Albemarle V1610 on display at the Lincolnshire Aviation Heritage Centre, East Kirkby, Lincolnshire.

Larger items recovered from V1610. (both Dave Stubley LARG)

By May of 1944 the reliability of the Albemarles was giving cause for concern, the situation being so critical that engineers from both Armstrong Whitworth and the engine manufacturer, Bristol, were called in to assess the situation. After an investigation it was discovered that the porcelain base of the Bristol Hercules' engine spark plugs were breaking up under the intense heat, causing engine failures. This could in part be attributed to the raising of cylinder head operating temperatures.

On July 24th 1944, Whitley Mk V BD230 from 42 OTU flew into high ground near the village of Muggington. The crew comprised of Flt. Sgt. John William Edward Cooper (Pilot), Sgt. William Brooksbank Smith (Bomb Aimer), Sgt. Henry Cowen (Navigator), Sgt. Walter Clifford Norcross (Wireless Operator) and Sergeant Maurice Mitchell Lyon (Air Gunner). All five crew were killed in the crash. Sergeant Smith was buried at Ashbourne cemetery whilst Sgt Lyon was buried at St Helen's cemetery in Lancashire. Today a fine memorial marks the crash site which is also the grave of the three other crew.

The memorial at the Muggington crash site of Whitley MkV BD230.
(Noel J Ryan, 2006)

It was not just the aircraft based at Ashbourne or Darley Moor which came to grief at the stations. On the1st August 1944, Canon Farrow, Vicar of St. Saviour Church in Ashbourne, was conducting a memorial service at Ashbourne airfield for the crew of Whitley BD230, which crashed at Mugginton. That same day, Vickers Wellington Mk. X HE993, from 18 OTU, RAF Finningley, crashed on Ashbourne airfield. The aircraft was burnt out and all the crew killed. The cause of the crash is unknown but the Station's ORB does mention the fact that there was heavy ground mist at the time.

It was not unusual for just about any aircraft to appear at short notice, or unannounced. Often the approach to an unfamiliar airfield, with a damaged aircraft, would result in a crash although this was not always the case. The ORB entry for Ashbourne, dated 9th September 1944 notes; "*Three Flying Fortress Aircraft made emergency landings at Ashbourne on return from operational duties. Aircraft based at RAF Station Polebrooke.*"

These aircraft were Boeing B-17Gs and belonged to the 351st Bomb Group, 1st Air Division of the US Army Eighth Air Force. The 351st Bomb Group was based at Polebrooke in Northamptonshire from April 1943 to June 1945. At the time of the Flying Fortresses arrival at Ashbourne, the Bomb Group was attacking enemy positions to cover *Operation Market Garden*, the ill-fated airborne assault to capture the bridges crossing the River Rhine.

.

Boeing B-17G Flying Fortresses of the 351st Bomb Group, 510th Bomb Sqn. The Group marking, a white J in a black triangle, is clearly visible. (U.S. Department of Defense).

Whilst the arrival of the B-17s was a successful recovery of aircraft which were returning from operations, the daily training schedule was to continue to claim victims.

Not all accidents and incidents could be attributed to the flying activities of the stations, as the following examples highlight. Landings could be just as hazardous as can be seen in the following two examples. Albemarle S. T. Mk. I Series. II P1659 on the 12th September 1944 suffered an undercarriage collapse on touch-down. Two months later on 21st November 1944 the undercarriage of Albemarle S. T. Mk. I Series II P1592 retracted itself on landing. Both aircraft were damaged beyond repair as a result of these crashes.

The crew of Albemarle S. T. Mk. II Series II, P1554, came to grief whilst attempting to land at Ashbourne on 18th December 1944, in what has become a famous incident locally. Whilst making its approach to the runway, the aircraft was too low and it crashed onto the roof of a large house named *The Mount* on New Road, Ashbourne, about one and a half miles north-west of the airfield. This resulted in the removal of the roof and upper floor of the dwelling. The navigator, P/O Bunting was killed in the crash whilst the pilot, Flt Lt Turner and crew members F/O Wardlow and Sgt. Rudge, were detained in the Station Sick Quarters. The fifth crew member, Sgt. Coleman was uninjured.

The Mount *as it is today, the missing upper half of the house being quite apparent. (Noel J Ryan, 2006)*

As the War in Europe came to a close, the need for crews was greatly reduced and with the final drawn down of 42 OTU, so the number of accidents reduced. The amount of flying hours the hard-pressed aircraft were expected to make, maintained by the equally hard-pressed ground crews, it is not surprising that so many tragic events took place. It is neither the fault of the aircraft, the crews (both ground and air) – rather, it was the extreme circumstances under which everything and everyone was expected to operate. It must have been with great relief that the War came to end.

6

28 MAINTENANCE UNIT, 1950 – 1954

Like so many airfields built during the War years, Ashbourne and Darley Moor, immediately after the cessation of hostilities in Europe, became disused for flying after having served their intended function. Still being retained by the RAF, the status of the airfields became that of 'Care and Maintenance', which consisted of the two sites being held to a minimum standard, to be reactivated again quickly should they be needed. Due to the rapid advance in aircraft designs and in particular the introduction of jet-powered front line military aircraft, this would mean that most of these 'duration only' airfields would never again be used for flying purposes by the RAF.

A new lease of life, which was to last as long as the stations' operational period in World War 2, was given to both Ashbourne and Darley Moor by the RAF when, in 1950, an element of 28 Maintenance Unit (MU) moved in. Number 28 MU was formed at Harpur Hill near Buxton in Derbyshire. Harpur Hill was a former limestone quarry which was owned by ICI, who sold it to the Air Ministry in 1938. The intention from the outset was to turn the quarry and surrounding countryside into a huge ordnance storage area and by 1940, it was indeed a fully operational facility. Bombs, missiles, gas canisters and by the late 1950s, nuclear weapons were all stored and maintained here. The camp was extended in the post-war period and remained operational until the early 1960s, when it was transferred to civilian ownership and further extended to a total of around 500 acres (202 hectares). It became part of the University of Derby and latterly became and testing a research facility for the Health and Safety Executive, who still use the site today in conjunction with the University of Sheffield.

With the outbreak of the Korean War, beginning in June 1950, the involvement of UK forces meant that the MUs were once again busy supplying ordnance for this campaign. As with so many other disused airfields, it was found that the available land afforded by the runways at both Ashbourne and Darley Moor provided excellent widely-dispersed areas of storage for bombs and missiles waiting to be serviced and forwarded on to the front line. The close proximity of Harpur Hill to both sites, with its excellent road and rail connections, meant that the two airfields were in an ideal position for this function.

Ashbourne Railway Station and Marshalling Yards at the time of 28 MU. (Steve Stancall)

One man, Steve Stancall, after passing an entrance examination and aptitude test, elected to spend his National Service in the RAF. Eventually, Steve was based at Harpur Hill as part of 28 MU, and was posted to RAF Ashbourne in late 1950. The RAF presence at the airfields during this time was small, with around twenty men of all ranks being billeted at RAF Ashbourne. The staff posted to Darley Moor commuted the few miles each day courtesy of the RAF Motor Transport section which was based at Ashbourne.

At regular intervals, a specially assigned train would arrive at Ashbourne from Harpur Hill amidst much security and would be laden with heavy ordnance for delivery and storage at Ashbourne or Darley Moor. All available personnel would then proceed with the unloading, a lengthy operation. This procedure was carried out by two or three lorry-mounted cranes. These would place the bombs onto Leyland *Hippo* lorries and bomb trailers of the type that were to be found on the airfield bomb dumps during the Second World War. The *Hippos*, once loaded, towed the bomb trailers, making their way up the hill to Ashbourne airfield and with the site being placed fairly high on the plateau to the south-east of the Town (with a steep gradient approaching it), the resultant climb could be fraught with problems and sometimes a little danger. One particular occasion, which Mr. Stancall remembers clearly, was of a munitions convoy making its way uphill out of the town. Shortly after leaving the railway station in Ashbourne, a bit of over zealous cornering saw a 2000lb bomb fall from its trailer and roll down Church Street, eventually coming to a stop in the Town. An air of silence was followed by a frantic rush of activity as the servicemen raced to recover the bomb before higher ranks became aware of what had happened. Despite several of the local inhabitants being around, no-one in authority was, apparently, ever the wiser to the incident!

Typical bomb stores scene, location unknown. (Chris Russell)

Once munitions were safely delivered to their destination at the top of the hill, the servicing of the ordnance was carried out in fuzing sheds erected on the runways, suitably spaced as a safety precaution. The bombs were in a poor state of repair, most having very rusty casings due to age. A lot of them were of American construction and had supposedly been checked at another location by the Americans themselves. However, as Mr. Stancall recollects, the 'checking' was carried out by way of driving past the bomb stacks in a Jeep and giving them a cursory visual inspection. This examination was confirmed by chalking a white cross on them. As Mr. Stancall quipped, these bombs came to Ashbourne "*...to be done properly...*"!

The servicing of these free-fall bombs consisted of cleaning the casings and checking the welded seams for signs of leakage of the explosive content. This was followed by the nose cone being removed and inspected. Once reassembled, the bomb would be deemed ready and placed with the others for storage and dispatch.

When enough ordnance of a particular type was ready, the reverse process would take place. The *Hippos* and bomb trailers, perhaps more carefully now, would wind their way down to the station to be loaded onto a train in the goods yard, again a lengthy and arduous process. Once loaded, the train would make its way to the end destination, Woolwich Arsenal in London. It was required that three men from 28 MU accompany the train in case of any incidents and Mr. Stancall carried out this escort duty on a number of occasions. The journey was long and was not helped by the train being repeatedly put in sidings or 'passing loops' to allow other, faster, non-military rail traffic through. Before the train could continue on its journey the whole load had to be inspected in case anything had become disturbed by a passing train. Once that had been done, they could continue until the next siding and so on until the journey's end.

For the journey down and the return, which was on a normal passenger service, the rations for the three men forming the escort party consisted of half a loaf of bread, a tin of 'bully beef', some butter and six eggs between them. The whole procedure of travelling to Woolwich, handing the ordnance over and returning on a normal service passenger train could take over twenty-four hours.

It was not just free fall bombs from the WW2 era that were present at Ashbourne and Darley Moor, other ordnance was also stored and serviced at the airfields. Rocket projectiles, detonators and even a hangar crammed full of seven inch hooded flares are all remembered, along with a large quantity of *Window* which was also kept at Ashbourne. This particular item was contained within structures in Bradley Wood, to the immediate north of the Ashbourne airfield site and in later years would become a plaything for the local boys. Local residents, John Watson and Gerry Williams, remember that at one time, the aluminum could be seen draped from tree to tree like some futuristic Christmas decoration!

Steve Stancall on a bomb train at Ashbourne in the early 1950s.
(Steve Stancall)

Another type of munition to be stored and serviced by 28 MU were depth charges. These charges had an unusual method of being checked. The end cap was removed and a length of wire with a bulb on the end was lowered inside, the purpose being to check the wax seals were intact and if necessary, reseal them. The aperture the bulb had to pass through was fractionally wider than the bulb itself, which would make a reasonable seal if left in the opening. On one occasion, a Sergeant was carrying out these inspections on some depth charges and taking the chance to pass on some instruction and advice to the attendant junior ranks. The arrival of the tea van saw all work cease as the servicemen took their break. What was not realised at the time was that, in his haste, the Sergeant had left the lit bulb just inside the inspection cap. Upon finishing their tea the Sergeant and his men returned to be greeted by a glowing red depth charge; the plugging of the gap and the heat given out had created a radiator effect. The bulb was hastily removed and eventually, the depth charge cooled down, leaving the Sergeants face as the only remaining red glow!

Once again, the incident was kept very much hushed up, the Commanding Officer and his staff being none the wiser. However, had there been an explosion, the 'top brass' at Harpur Hill would certainly have heard about it!

One pastime which, although short-lived, was a great source of amusement for some of the bored staff and involved the use of surplus detonators. A good game for the men was to split into teams and like some strange snowball fight, start throwing them at each other! The tedious task was to search for these devices, picking them all up. Inevitably not all were recovered and many remained lying around. Eventually and perhaps predictably, a local came across one and picked it up and his lack of handling experience resulted in it exploding, causing serious burns. This time the higher authorities *did* hear about the incident. As result, all leave was cancelled for a week and the servicemen spent their free time on hands and knees scouring the airfield for detonators!

Despite the presence of the RAF Police at both sites, the handling crews still had to perform their share of guard duty, usually a twenty-four hour stint. On one occasion, the area of the airfield around Bradley Wood had become an unofficial home for some travellers and they had tied their horses to some trees, not far from the threshold of the north/south runway. Whilst patrolling the area, one of the guardsmen was amazed to see that the horses had freed themselves and were happily grazing in amongst the piles of bombs, using the bomb stacks as 'scratching posts' and generally, as Mr Stancall remembers "*knocking them about*". The travellers were removed the next day.

As in most occupations, the men from 28 MU were always happy to exploit any potential perks, particularly if there was a chance of any extra curricular earning potential. A group of airmen, whilst in Ashbourne town, were approached by a farmer from Darley Moor. The farmer had just bought a redundant railway carriage for storage purposes, which was still located at Ashbourne railway station. Could they, for a spot of remuneration, use their cranes and lorries to transport the carriage? The answer was "*yes*" and having completed the removal, the men were paid twenty-five pounds each, a fair sum in the early 1950s. Once again, all this happened without the knowledge of the 'powers that be'. Apparently, the carriage remains on the farm to this day, although its exact whereabouts is now unknown.

In 1952 Steve Stancall left Ashbourne and Darley Moor, returned to Buxton and from there, a posting away. The storage and servicing of ordnance at the two sites continued until 1954. This time the RAF flag was lowered for the last time, the airfields once again becoming disused, this time permanently. With the end of the Korean conflict, the run-down of both stations was rapid. Facilities were dismantled or demolished, trees planted on former dispersed sites and the runways either shortened or broken up completely. The land was sold off or found its way back into the hands of those from whom it had been requisitioned in 1941 and the sites took on the forlorn air of abandonment.

7

1954 TO THE PRESENT

The departure of 28 MU in 1954 heralded the end of the Royal Air Force's tenure at both Ashbourne and Darley Moor. An air of neglect hung over the two airfields as they, like many more throughout the country were left to the elements, vandalism and dereliction, before new uses could be found for them.

Ashbourne airfield, with its hangars and extensive Technical Site infrastructure, along with its proximity to the town of Ashbourne, would see the development of industry and related trades. These would include haulage, storage, and light industry and a limited amount of private flying. The Communal Site would later become a caravan and camping site, with many structures surviving today. Darley Moor, on the other hand, was rapidly dismantled, reverting largely to agriculture and in the case of its dispersed sites, plantation woodland would come to dominate.

ASHBOURNE

Ashbourne, being the parent airfield and designed as a heavy bomber site in its original inception, was equipped with a more robust infrastructure in terms of airfield Technical Site buildings and hangars. The runways, perimeter tracks and most of the buildings survived for many years. Private flying took place using light aircraft, especially during the late 1960s and into the mid-1970s. Aside from general aviation in light civil aircraft, further specialist instruction and courses in parachute training were also offered.

Throughout the war years, Ashbourne saw a number of aircraft come to grief on the airfield or in the vicinity. All aircrew in World War 2 were issued with parachutes as an aid to life preservation, most of these being supplied by the Irvin Company at their Icknield Way and Spirella factories in Letchworth, Hertfordshire. The choice of either having the parachute strapped on to the body or having it close by was largely dictated by the relative crew position (especially in a bomber), and the restrictions in terms of space. Generally, the pilot, navigator and engineer would be able to wear their parachutes but crew members such as rear gunners could not. In times of crisis, with the need to leave a possibly spinning and falling aircraft, it was almost impossible to overcome centrifugal forces. With the aircraft possibly burning, the inability to locate the parachute, strap it on and bale out of the stricken aircraft led to the loss of many aircrew. The ones who did manage to bale out would find themselves members of an exclusive group called *The Caterpillar Club.*

The *Irvin Airchutes* company director, Leslie Irvin, founded the *Caterpillar Club* in 1922, the intention being to honour all those whose lives had been saved by a parachute. The Company administered applications to the Club and members received a certificate and a Golden Caterpillar brooch. Membership was open to anyone saved by any parachute and not necessarily an Irvin-type. A running total of *Caterpillar* badges awarded was kept at the Spirella factory as a means of boosting staff morale and by the end of the War in Europe, this stood at 20,538 Allied aircrew members!

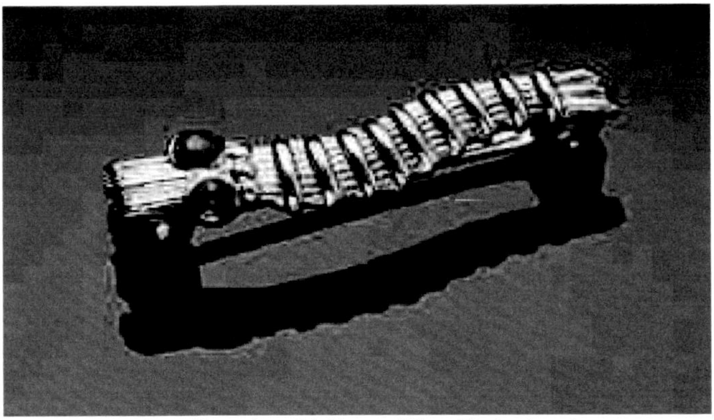

The official gold Caterpillar Club *tie pin*
(Airborne Systems/Irvin Caterpillar Club)

Saturday the 18th October 1975, would see another airman operating from Ashbourne obtain the prestigious *Caterpillar* honour. At this time, parts of the airfield were being used for the training of sports parachutists. One aircraft used for the task was Cessna 182E Skylane G-ARWL (de-registered by the UK Civil Aviation Authority in 1976), which was in the air flying circuits prior to the commencement of scheduled parachute training jumps. On board was Ken Miller (pilot), Derek Schofield (jump master), Peter Denley (instructor) and students Frances Ives and Stewart Avent.

Cessna 182E Skylane G-ARWL, used by the parachutists at Ashbourne

(A. J. Jackson Collection)

The Cessna reached its allotted altitude and heading, the students preparing themselves for their jump. The first student (Ives) exited without incident with Stewart Avent being the next in line to go. As he approached the open door of the aircraft, Avent quickly went through his checks and recalled the instructions he had been given. He steadied himself and prepared to follow the first student out of the Cessna. As he jumped, his parachute pack became entangled in the aircraft's step and undercarriage - Avent was now left dangling outside the aircraft. The resultant interruption to the airflow over the tail empennage caused the Cessna to react severely causing Ken Miller to struggle to maintain control of G-ARWL. Jump master Schofield made his way to the Cessna's open door and attempted to free the unfortunate student but before Schofield could reach him, Avent himself assumed he was now free of the aircraft and released his *reserve* parachute.

As the reserve parachute inflated in the slipstream, all control of the Cessna was lost and the pilot was powerless to prevent it falling to earth. However, both bizarrely and fortunately, the inflation of the reserve parachute actually *slowed* the aircraft's descent somewhat, with Avent attached somewhere outside. The aircraft came to the ground inverted, on the north-eastern side of the airfield (fortunately onto the soft ground used by JCB for testing excavators!). All on board were very lucky to survive and amazingly, a photographer, Eddie McBride, was on hand to record the incident.

The front page of a local Sunday newspaper the next day showed the photograph of the Cessna coming down, nose first and partially inverted, suspended under Stewart Avent's reserve parachute. The headline proudly proclaimed "*Hero parachutist saves stricken aircraft!*" The article went on to explain that when the Cessna's engine stalled, Avent held onto the fuselage and inflated his parachute, thus saving all their lives! Stewart Avent suffered a sprained back and the others involved received a range of injuries from cuts to multiple fractures. Pilot Ken Miler was later awarded a *Gold Caterpillar* pin by the Irvin Company (now

Airborne Systems, USA); he was the only one who had boarded the aircraft without the intention to leave by parachute, unlike the students, who had travelled aloft with intention of doing so. Whilst he did not leave the aircraft, his life was nonetheless, saved by one. This event, therefore, qualified him for the award!

(right) The inflated parachute of Stuart Avent, along with the Cessna, just above the ground

(below) The aftermath of this rather bizarre, and fortunately non-fatal, incident

(Eddie McBride via BPA, 1975)

Many local people had become increasingly concerned about noise pollution and safety prompting a number of complaints. The incident with G-ARWL and the parachute seemed to vindicate the people who were raising these objections. As a result of this, Derbyshire Dales District Council gave the parachute club notice to cease operating.

Like many other disused airfields, the potential for utilizing the site for industrial purposes was being realised by Derbyshire Dales District Council. From 1975 onwards, there began a steady process of demolishing the existing airfield buildings which were in the way of industrial development. The T2 hangars, because of their dimensions and construction, made ideal warehouse and storage facilities and three of Ashbourne's four T2 hangars on the former Technical Site remained for this purpose. The fourth T2 hangar on the north-western perimeter track was dismantled, although its base remains today.

The control tower survived post-war, being used as offices for one of the many business which began to occupy the expanding industrial site, although this was demolished in 2004. The process of turning the airfield into an Industrial Estate was gradual but continuous and by the middle of the 1990s, a multitude of modern buildings occupied the former Technical Site on the south and western extremities of the airfield site itself.

Ashbourne's main entrance 1975. (Malcolm L Giddings)

Ashbourne Communal Site prior to the caravan park.
(Malcolm L Giddings, 1975)

The substantial concrete runways made ideal bases for prefabricated buildings and many of these have been erected on the southern section of the subsidiary north-south runway. The western end of the east-west runway has been lost amongst the industrial units. The remaining runway is the former main south-east/north-west strip and it too has lost its north-western end, being used as the foundations for further units.

The current status of the runway. (Noel J. Ryan, 2005)

View down the main runway at Ashbourne (32/14: north-west/south-east) (Noel J Ryan, 2006)

When the main runway is viewed, either from the ground or air, it is difficult to believe that it remains active towards the south-eastern end. Several light aircraft and helicopters are stored in a more recent hangar and regularly use this runway. One of the pilots who lives locally, businessman Richard McLachlan (who operates a Robinson R-22 Beta II), confirms that take-offs from this surface can be interesting! The runway is swept a few times during the year and generally kept free from weeds and any other foreign objects detrimental to aircraft. During 2005, planning permission was granted to Vital Earth for the construction of a 'green' composting and peat-free growing media production facility and is now built and fully operational. The airfield is still used for private flying by the light aircraft based here.

Also operating from the site is the Derbyshire Radio Control Flyers Model Aero Club, making use of a section of one of the runways for their activities. If full size aircraft do have to vacate Ashbourne in the future then perhaps, because of the scale model activities, a link with aviation will endure.

The Robinson R-22 Beta II G-BYCF, owned and operated by Richard McLachlan. (Chris Percy, 2006)

In this age of ever-increasing housing development coupled with a shortage of available land, inevitably some 'new-build' properties have appeared to the north-west of the airfield site at

Ashbourne. This has been a feature of other disused airfields, one of the most prominent of these being the former RAF Skellingthorpe airfield near Lincoln. This airfield has been completely taken over by housing estate developments, although its past has been remembered with the appropriate naming of some roads and the erection of two memorials, one of which is very substantial. Unfortunately at Ashbourne, this opportunity has been lost, the only connection being the Industrial Estate; the name of the Industrial Estate itself and two of the service roads, which have been named after two 42 OTU's resident aircraft types, the Blenheim (Blenheim Road) and the Whitley (Whitley Way).

DARLEY MOOR

The return of farming activities at Darley Moor saw much of the airfield reverting to agriculture. The sale of the land back to any original owners was sometimes at a lower price than was originally paid immediately prior to the airfield's construction. The Technical Site buildings and much of the accommodation were soon demolished, making way for plantation woodland. With the exception of the instructional buildings to the immediate west of the airfield, the rest of the site would be cleared.

The surviving flight hut at Darley Moor in the late 1970s. (Malcolm L. Giddings)

Darley Moor Guardroom in the 1970s. (Malcolm L Giddings)

The now-demolished Operations Block at Darley Moor in the 1970s. (Malcolm L. Giddings)

Inside the Operations Block sometime in the 1970s. (Malcolm L Giddings)

The presence of the surviving runways and perimeter track attracted the attention of a group of individuals keen on motorcycle racing, their plan being to set up a racing circuit using the existing concrete. The fact that at most airfields the runways were joined by a continuous perimeter track made disused airfields more or less ready-made motor racing circuits. Many of todays more famous motor racing circuits were originally World War II airfields; Goodwood (formerly RAF Westhampnett, west

Sussex), Snetterton (formerly RAF Snetterton Heath, Norfolk) and Silverstone (formerly RAF Silverstone, Northamptonshire) are just three examples.

In 1965, after a short but bitter legal struggle, planning consent for one practice day and five race meetings per year launched Darley Moor into the British motorcycle sporting scene. There were many objections from various quarters and some of the planning conditions imposed were, at best, restrictive. The Club, despite objections locally, overcame all the problems and racing commenced in 1965. During March 1967, after several more legal battles, the bridleway and footpaths were closed across the areas of the site where the motorsport was to take place (primarily at the northern end of the airfield) and the Council planning authority agreed to allow the Club to run race meetings on five Sundays and three other days between March and October each year, for the next seven years.

The Club gradually established itself on the motorcycle-racing calendar and over time facilities were improved, as was the state of the track itself. In 1974, the Club and its landlords, with assistance from the County Council, reinstated the bridle and footpaths subject to the Club's right to close them during any activity on the circuit. This condition still applies today, although the Club has always allowed people to walk the footpaths, even on race days, providing marshals to escort walkers across the circuit between races. The planning consent was also renewed that year for a further seven years. There would still be many problems and obstacles to overcome in the years ahead and even today, it operates under various conditions and restrictions imposed upon it.

The Club now operates as the Darley Moor Motor Cycle Road Race Club (Darley Moor MCRRC) Ltd. and is only responsible for the areas of the airfield where racing takes place.

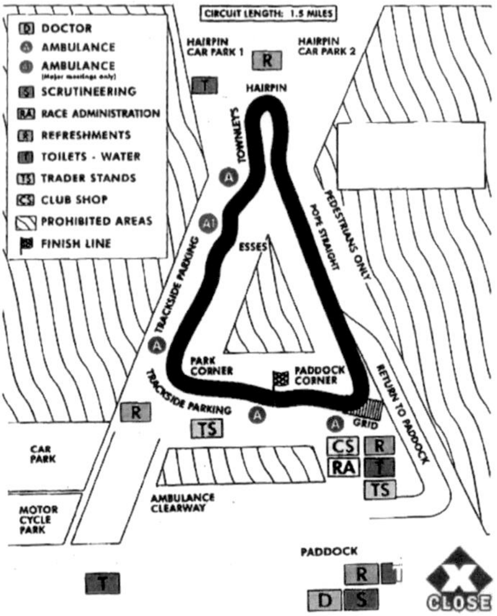

Map of Darley Moor racing circuit. (Darley Moor MCRRC Ltd)

Many years after the RAF moved out flying activities still continue at Darley Moor airfield. (Chris Percy, 2006)

The southern end of Darley Moor airfield, whilst being returned to agriculture, has over the years also seen a steady return to flying activities. Microlight flying and instruction, para-gliding and parachuting can all be seen, when the weather permits, on the area south of the reinstated Wyaston Road, utilizing the former perimeter track and the grassed areas in between.

THE AIRFIELDS TODAY – THE VISIBLE REMAINS

What can the enthusiast or just curious visitor expect to see of the two former RAF Stations today? A knowledge of what was there originally will aid interpretation of what remains now. Airfield record site plans, originally produced by the Air Ministry (copies of which are held at the Royal Air Force Museum, Hendon), can provide invaluable information regarding the buildings and their original layout.

RAF ASHBOURNE

Starting at Ashbourne, the A52 Derby Road climbs away from the Town to the high plateau that the airfield occupies. As the road levels out, the entrance to the Industrial Estate is on the left. This is not the original main entrance to the station, which was a little further on, close to the location of the roundabout of the new By-pass. The entrance which gives access to the Industrial Estate now, would, if access could have been gained that way onto the airfield during its operational life, take you past a couple of maintenance blocks and a salvage building, all long gone.

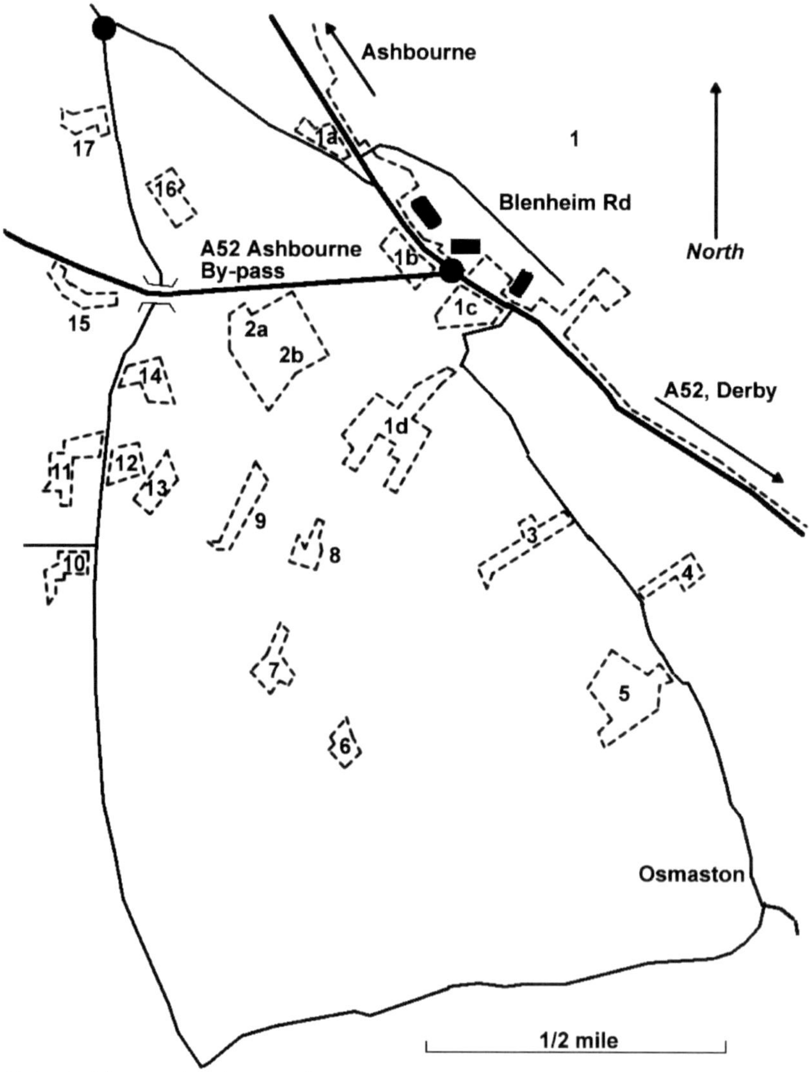

RAF Ashbourne's Dispersed Sites.
(adapted by C. Percy from A/M Drawing No. 1117/45)

Map Key

1 - 1d) Airfield Site, Technical & Instructional Sites
2a) WAAF Dormitory Site
2b) RAF Communal Site
3) RAF Site No. 6
4) H. F. D. F. Site
5) WAAF Communal Site
6) Sewage Disposal Site
7) RAF Site No. 8
8) RAF Site No. 5
9) RAF Site No. 10
10) RAF Site No. 2
11) RAF Site No. 9
12) W. T. Site
13) RAF Site No. 3
14) Station Sick Quarters
15) RAF Site No. 1
16) RAF Site No. 4
17) RAF Site No. 7

Stained glass window inside the Mess on the Communal Site, RAF Ashbourne.

(Paul Stanley/Peak Gateway Caravan Park, 2006)

Following the road to the right, note the new housing estate occupying the south-western area of the airfield on the left. As the road straightens up, you are now on what was formally the south-western perimeter track. Between this and the Derby road stood the Technical Site area. Look left for the "Blenheim Veterinary Surgery". Continuing straight along this former taxiway, on the right can be glimpsed the side of Hangar 2, one of three surviving at Ashbourne. The site of the Watch Tower, or in modern terms Control Tower is now approached, just before the trees to the right in front of the modern unit was its location, now demolished without trace. It is hard to imagine now but around 60 years ago, training aircraft would be making their way along this perimeter track, past the Control Tower and on, towards the head of the runway, ready to take off on yet another mission. Today, the aero-engines are replaced by the diesel engines of the many vehicles using the Industrial Estate. Also in this area were the Parachute Store, the Fire Tender shed and a variety of other buildings whose functions were essential to the running of the Station.

The location of the Watch Office. (Chris Percy, 2006)

The former perimeter track, now Blenheim Road, *with modern units occupying the former Technical Site. (Chris Percy, 2006)*

Carrying on along the road, the site of the technical area to the right is now a plethora of modern warehouses and other buildings. To the left, sixty years ago the visitor would be looking across onto the main runway but now it is hidden behind another mass of modern buildings. One of the service roads to these has been named *Whitley Way*, a small reminder of times past.

Industrial Estate Road Sign, Whitley Way, *a link to the Armstrong Whitworth Whitleys once so familiar here. (Noel J Ryan, 2006)*

Continuing along the perimeter track, the journey is brought to an abrupt end by the presence of mesh fencing. Looking straight ahead, some hangars can be seen; these are not original and are built on the southern end of the north-south runway. Following, by eye, the course of this runway to the left, its junction with the main runway may just be seen.

Looking over the flying field and the area of the three runways it is hard to imagine that this place echoed day and night with the sounds of large aero-engines. On the right, at the far end of the former Technical Site Hangar 4 is visible. To the left of this, although nothing now remains, was one of the airfield's mounted searchlights.

Hangar No. 4, RAF Ashbourne. (Chris Percy, 2006)

Turning around and back-tracking to the Industrial Estate entrance, off to the left, a wide strip of concrete can be seen. A short distance further along brings you to the last remaining hangar (No. 3) at Ashbourne. This is now re-clad and it is the least recognisable of the three remaining hangars.

Return to the main entrance to the Industrial Estate and the junction with the main Derby Road. Turning left out of this junction, Preston's garage can be seen on the right. This existed during the airfields' operational life (although now much modified from its wartime appearance) as a local landmark to the aircrews, especially those taking off from, or returning to, the east-west runway.

Carrying on south-east along the Derby road, the next point of interest is upon us, alongside the roundabout that the new by-pass used to avoid Ashbourne town centre. To the left near here was the guardhouse and the main entrance to the airfield, which both existed until at least 1998.

The former main entrance and Guard Room & Fire Party Room at RAF Ashbourne alongside the A52, seen in 1998. This has since been demolished, with only the concrete floor remaining. (Chris Percy)

On the far side of the road, again completely demolished, were a further two sites associated with the operational side of the airfield. The first of these, which was slightly before the main entrance on the other side of the road, housed the Motor Transport (MT) section which also held a large fuel compound and service shed. As the name suggests, this was essentially a large garage for maintaining the many different vehicles which the airfield required. The second site was the nerve centre of the operational side of the station and was located between the new roundabout and the minor road that drops down to Osmaston. Here was the Operations Block, Station Offices and Photographic Block, all highly sensitive and secure areas. Had Ashbourne been used as a bomber base, from here the nightly bombing raids would have been orchestrated. As the Osmaston road junction is passed on the right, to the left can be seen two surviving brick-rendered huts, or at least parts of them. These buildings were the Towed Target Store and the Gas Clothing, Respirator Store and Workshop. The remains of these are now in private gardens.

The Gas Clothing, Respirator Store and Workshop. (Noel J Ryan, 2006)

A little further on the left there is an accessible path (Snipesmoor Lane). Following this between the houses will give a nice side view of Hangar 4 on the right. One of the aircraft hard-standing areas was also at this location, a little closer to the road next to the hangar. Rejoining the main road heading towards Derby, the next point of interest can be seen. A Pair of more recent metal-clad storage buildings are to the left - look over the hedgerow here. This is the view up the subsidiary north-south runway. The sheds are those which were visible from the mesh fencing at the end of the perimeter track inside the Industrial Estate.

The north-south runway remains, viewed from the southern end, alongside the A52. (Noel J. Ryan, 2006)

The same north-south runway, viewed from the air, looking south. (Noel J Ryan, 2005)

Looking to the right, a derelict hut and the base of another can be seen. These are the remains of "A" flight crew rooms, workshops and squadron offices, the latter being destroyed when an Albemarle skidded of the runway due to a tyre bursting whilst landing from the north. Unfortunately, several WAAFs were killed in the crash.

The remains of the "A" flight squadron huts, close to the southern end of the north-south runway. (Noel J Ryan, 2006)

Continue along the Derby Road (A52), a cross roads is encountered. This is the junction of the A15 and the previously-closed Lady Hole Lane. Turning left here and travelling along this a strip of concrete perimeter track can now be seen on the left and a little further along, the end of the main runway running north-west to south-east . This is runway number 3 in the original terminology or, more accurately, the threshold of runway 32 (320°).

The south-eastern end of the main runway which ran southeast – northwest. Note the reinstated Lady Hole Lane, running across the centre of the photograph, bisecting the runway. This runway is still used occasionally for flying. (Noel J Ryan, 2005)

Looking to the right (south-east), across the road, are the last few yards of this runway a short distance on, to the right, is a further stretch of perimeter track, linking the runway head to the rest of the airfield. A short walk along here, the perimeter track curves to the right, eventually opening up to a wide expanse of concrete, and this is the start of the main runway.

From here the Blenheims, Whitleys, Albemarles would have wound up their engines against the brakes. The whole aircraft would be shuddering, the pilot waiting for the signal to take off from the controller's caravan. Behind the aircraft, the grass would be flattened in the propeller wash, perhaps reaching as far back as the main runway beacon, several yards from the threshold. The signal received and brakes released , the aircraft would make its way down the runway looking for flight.

Continuing a little further along this section of perimeter track, with the runway on the right, some concrete may be noticed disappearing into the undergrowth on the left. This was the access to a further two aircraft hard-standings. Returning to the reinstated road and looking northwest gives a view over the airfield site. Part of the area to the right is the JCB testing complex and is private land.

The perimeter track at the head of the main runway, the aircraft dispersals are in the trees ahead. (Noel J Ryan, 2005)

Ashbourne had a number of dispersed communal and living accommodation sites and it is possible to take a circular tour around these to view what remains today (be it actual buildings or the now empty fields which these sites occupied). Start by taking the Osmaston Road from the A52 near the former Main Entrance, a junction is soon encountered. The road itself bears to the left, carrying straight on, along a former Air Ministry Road, the Peak Gateway Caravan Park is reached. Looking left and a the large building in the field, part of the former Instructional Site, is evident, the Gunnery and Crew Procedure Building. The Peak Gateway Caravan Park is built on the remains of the RAF Communal Site and is private property.

Peak Gateway Caravan Park viewed from the air. This was the former Communal Site. The A52 Ashbourne By-pass can be seen running left to right across the top of the photograph, through what was some the area once occupied by the WAAF Dormitory Site. (Noel J Ryan, 2006)

As the name suggests, this was where social activities, amongst the stations personnel would take place (the WAAFs having their own site some distance away). Facilities here included the Squash Court, Ablutions blocks, Institute and NAAFI, Grocery and Barbers Shops, Ration Store, Gymnasium and Chancel amongst others. The Officer's Mess is now the camp restaurant and public bar, the gymnasium and chancel survive, as do the squash courts, all of which have been renovated and are currently in use as camp site buildings. The Commanding Officer's Quarters are still standing - a long building to the rear of the Gymnasium and Chancel. The northern-most parts of this site have been lost to the recently-built A52 (Ashbourne) By-pass and its cutting.

Looking left (south), the area appears to be a mass of caravans but a walk around reveals many concrete bases of former buildings, including airmen's dining rooms and the Institute and NAAFI .

The Commanding Officers Quarters. (Noel J Ryan, 2006)

The Gymnasium and Chancel (rear). (Noel J Ryan, 2006)

The Squash Court. (Noel J Ryan, 2006)

One structure, due to its design and construction, often to be found remaining on former communal sites, is the Standby Set House. This was a substantial brick building which housed two emergency diesel or oil fired generators. Should the main electricity supply fail, these would provide an emergency supply for the site. At Ashbourne, the surviving Standby Set House can be found at the southern end of the caravan site.

Standby Set House. (Chris Percy, 2005)

Rejoining the road at the Peak Gateway entrance, turning right, the journey continues towards Osmaston, along Moor Lane. On the right can be seen the front of the Instructional Site building noted whilst entering the caravan park. Also on this site would have been the Link Trainers and A.M. Bombing and Gunnery Trainers, as well as other support buildings, all geared towards the ground training required to complete the courses.

The Gunnery and Crew Procedure building from the air. (Noel J Ryan, 2006)

Continuing to Osmaston, a short distance to the right was the former RAF Site Number 6 in the trees to the right of the road. This contained the living quarters for Officers and Airmen in the form of Nissen or Maycrete-type huts. A few yards further on, to the left (opposite two natural ponds), was the entrance to the H.F.D.F site. The entrances to these fields are now the only indication that these sites ever existed. A little further on to the right can be seen a wide area of trees with an access track at the far side of the woods, near to the church. This was the WAAF Communal and Living Quarters Site. Similar facilities to those of the RAF Communal Site were provided; dining rooms, Officer's Mess and Bathhouse, Laundry and the Station Sick Quarters. The former access track is a public right of way and a few building floors and blast shelters can be made out in the woods to the left (west) of the path. Caution must be exercised as the area is overgrown, hiding numerous open drains.

One of seven Air Raid Shelters which survive on the WAAF Communal Site, near Osmaston. (Chris Percy, 2007)

Four of Ashbourne's dispersed sites, viewed towards the north-north-west. The main airfield is visible to the top right, with the now heavily developed Technical Site to the left. (Noel J. Ryan, 2006)

Continuing through Osmaston, Moor Lane becomes Quilow Lane as it curves to the right (west). From here, after one mile, take the first right turn, near Osmaston pastures. The road now heads north and straightens up. There were several former living sites along this road, which heads back into Ashbourne. RAF Site 2 is the first to be encountered on the left (half a mile after the previous junction, two hundred yards past Moor Lane Farm on the left), again a mix of Officer's and Airmen's quarters. Lying across the fields to the right were another four RAF sites, numbers 3, 10, 5 and 8 respectively, all being a mix of barrack rooms and quarters. Some Air Ministry trackways (now used as access to the fields), and the odd building base and blast shelter survive on these sites, which are on private land.

Turning northwards, a long building of rendered brick construction can be seen, intact, in a field on the right and to its left, a surviving blast shelter. This was the Wireless Transmitter (W/T) Site and surrounding it were six transmitting masts.

The Wireless Transmitter building. (Noel J Ryan, 2006)

The Wireless Transmitter site blast shelter. (Noel J Ryan, 2006)

Across the road from the W/T site was a further accommodation site, RAF Site 9, which again contained an assortment of quarters and barrack blocks. The northern-most part of this site contained a Bulk Fuel Compound, measuring 90 feet by 54 feet.

The site just about visible from the road to the right, before the new By-pass bridge, was the location of the Station Sick Quarters (now a private house). This was linked by a trackway to the Communal Site and WAAF Dormitory Site, a short distance to the east.

Further on the Wyaston Road, on the right (now completely obliterated by the By-pass cutting), was the location of RAF Site 1. Still continuing towards Ashbourne, the road goes under the new By-pass bridge, emerging into a newly-built housing estate . In this area were the last two remaining sites, RAF Site Nos. 4 and 7. Site 4 was on the right, in the area of Willow Meadow Road and the school, meanwhile Site 7 was a little further along, to the left around the current location of Premier Avenue, near to Leys Farm and are totally obliterated y the recent developments. These are the last buildings to be encountered associated with RAF Ashbourne.

The Station Sick Quarters at Ashbourne.
(Noel J Ryan, 2006)

RAF Darley Moor

Travelling south from Ashboune along the A515, the first indication of the existence of RAF Darley Moor is the sign for the motor racing track on the left. Before arriving here, the road has passed through the extreme eastern end of what was a mass of communal sites. Rather than being widely dispersed, as at Ashbourne, these were grouped together, almost as a conurbation, with little distribution. The new A515 at this point does not reflect the cartography of the original RAF site plans, its course having been altered significantly and now cuts straight through the middle of the former Communal and Number 2 Sites, to rejoin the original road layout south near Sites 5 and 6. Very little remains of these dispersed sites. To the west of this area were the other living sites clustered around Collycroft Farm and Gravel Pit Covert. A further site was over to the east in woods off of the minor road to the north of Edlaston village. Apart from a couple of blast shelters, all other traces of these sites has vanished.

Returning to the entrance of the racing circuit (the former Main Entrance to the airfield), a number of buildings may be seen. Please note that there is no access other than on race days, when an entrance fee is levied.

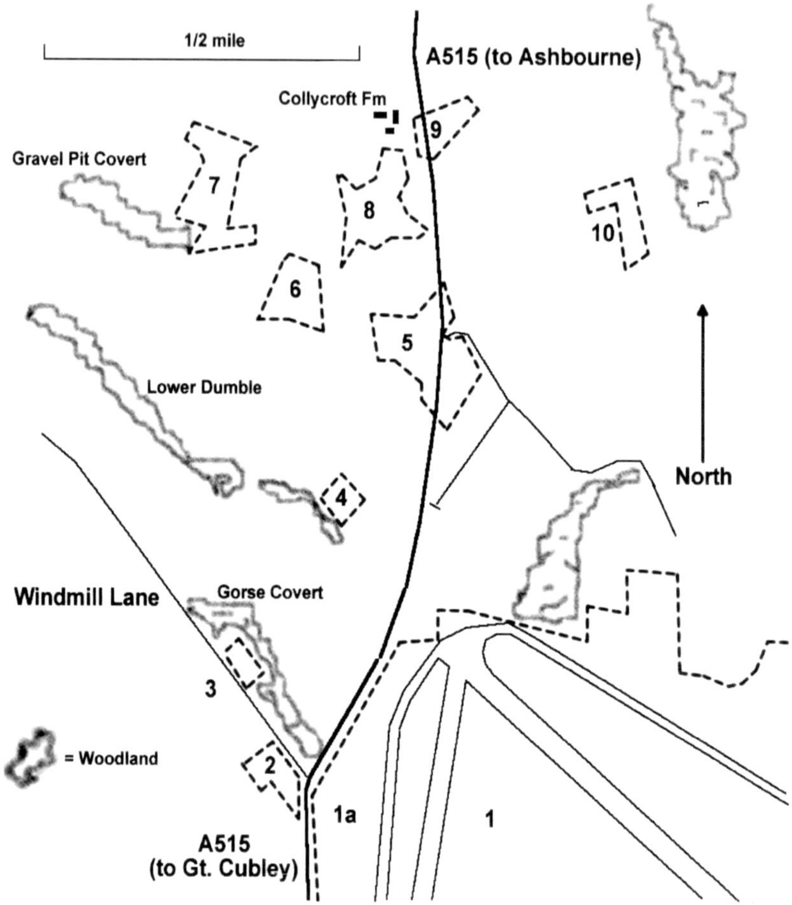

Figure 4: RAF Darley Moor Dispersed Sites. The line of the current A515 through the area is evident. (adapted by C. Percy from A/M Drawing No. 330/45)

Map Key

1 – 1a) Airfield & Technical Site
2) Instructional Site
3) Station Headquarters Site
4) Sewage Disposal Site
5) RAF Communal Site
6) WAAF Quarters & Communal Site
7) RAF Site No. 4
8) RAF Site No. 5
9) RAF Site No. 6
10) RAF Site No. 7

The former Main Entrance to RAF Darley Moor. (Chris Percy, 1998)

Through the entrance, to the right was the Airfield Site No. 1, the Technical Site, located between the western perimeter track and the A515. Buildings in this area included crew and flight offices, locker and drying rooms, squadron offices, motor transport sheds, the fire tender shed and the Watch Tower (control tower). To the left of the entrance was a group of ten buildings belonging to the Airfield Defence Unit and here, a few hut bases and the Sergeant's Latrine block survive.

One of the few remaining buildings on the Airfield Site, the Sergeant's Latrine block. (Chris Percy, 1998)

Continuing south, Windmill Lane runs west from the A515 to Snelston, where some of the best remaining buildings of RAF Darley Moor can be seen. Here, the Instructional Site remains virtually intact, although some buildings have been converted. This area, as can be seen from the annotated aerial photograph, contained two ground instructional buildings, a link trainer, bombing teacher and turret instruction building, as well as a latrine and picket post. Two blast shelters were also provided. The bombing teacher and turret building has now been converted to a house but is still recognizable for what it was. The picket post is now a garage or storage shed. Please note that these buildings are on private property and whilst they can be viewed from the road, permission for any photography must be sought.

The Bombing Trainer and Turret Teacher building, converted into a house. (Noel J Ryan, 2005)

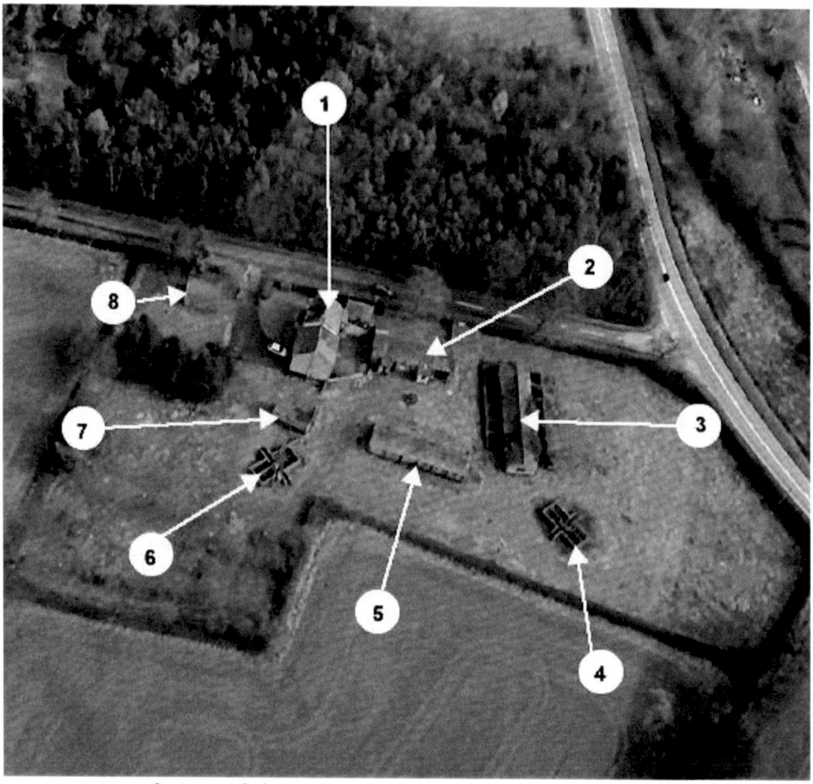

Aerial view of the Instructional Site at RAF Darley Moor.
(Chris Percy, 2006)

Instructional Site - Key
1) Bombing Trainer and Turret Teacher building
2) Link Trainer building
3) Ground Instructional building
4) Blast shelter
5) Ground Instructional building
6) Blast shelter
7) Latrines
8) Picket Post

The Link Trainer building. (Chris Percy, 2005)

A short distance along this road in, private woodland, to the right used to stand the remains of the Headquarters Site. As of 2007, the Operations Block has been demolished, the site now being the Woodland Caravan Park.

The Operations Block, now demolished to make way for a caravan site. (Noel J. Ryan, 2005)

Returning to the A515, turn south and then east, along the unclassified road towards Yeaveley. This road was closed during the operational life of the airfield as it was bisected by the southern end of the main north-south runway. Travelling down this minor road, the remains of the main runway and perimeter track are visible. Access may be gained along sections of this but it is restricted on race days at Darley Moor. To the right (south) the main runway and grass are used for flying of another type as the microlights and hang-gliders of Airways Airsports and others operate from here.

The main runway, viewed towards the north, from the minor road to Hales Green and Yeaveley, which now crosses the airfield, east of the A515. (Chris Percy, 2006)

Flying north up the main runway. (Chris Percy, 2006)

There is a further point of interest along this road: as the eastern perimeter track of the main runway is passed, a short distance on to the right, a track of concrete can be seen disappearing into a field. This is a relic of RAF Darley Moor's Bomb Dump service road.

The Bomb Dump service road, to the south of the unclassified road from the A515 leading to Hales Green and Yeaveley. (Chris Percy, 2005)

Returning back along this reinstated road, to the junction of the A515 which runs parallel to the main runway, two buildings, one with a ridged roof-line and the other, a flat-roofed structure, can be glimpsed to the left through the hedge alongside the road. These buildings, along with a low walled enclosure, were part of the 48,000 gallon Aviation Fuel Storage Installation. The hut base visible nearest the access track was the Picket Post for this location. These are the last visible remains at Darley Moor to be seen today.

The Bulk aviation fuel storage installation, seen from the A515. (Chris Percy, 2005)

Aerial view of the aviation fuel storage area (1) picket post and (2) bulk fuel storage compound. (Chris Percy, 2006)

D.C.O.

After a successful operational sortie it was customary to put the comment *D.C.O.* in the Flight Authorisation Book. The initials stand for *Duty Carried Out.* In terms of the duties assigned to the Stations of Ashbourne and Darley Moor, the phrase could very well be applied.

Beginning life as prospective bomber airfields and varied, often rapid changes of Command both Stations and their personnel managed their tasks admirably. With sometimes elderly aircraft to begin with and frequently inclement weather, the courses continued for three years of hostilities. With the arrival of large numbers of Whitleys and the Albermarle, critical training was undertaken under sometimes difficult circumstances and with these aircraft, these difficulties could be overcome. The turnover of crews being posted to the front-line units of 38 Group provided a valuable asset to many of the airborne operations in the latter stages of World War 2.

Neither airfield was the subject of Enemy attack throughout the War but that did not stop the sadness at the loss of crews in accidents and those lost operationally but it was not all sadness. Friendships were forged and even marriages which last to this day.

The continued use of the sites for a military purpose ensured some longevity to the two airfield's and the link with aviation is not lost today. Sport, leisure and business flying, along with model aircraft all keep the link with past alive. Current owners of various parts of the airfields commemorate their use in the names of roads and businesses and for the foreseeable future at least, the former airfields of RAF Ashbourne and RAF Darley Moor seems safe.

At the time of writing, there is no permanent, public memorial at either site. The memorial to the men and women who served here are the remains of the airfields themselves and the few surviving dispersed buildings, scattered away from the main sites.
It can be truly said that they could be described as having carried out their duty – and still continue to do so, this time for more peaceful purposes.

Bibliography

A/M Drawing Number 330/45 RAF Darley Moor – Airfield & Dispersed Sites, Record Site Plan (RAF Museum, Hendon)

A/M Drawing Number 1116/45 RAF Ashbourne – Airfield Site, Record Site Plan (RAF Museum, Hendon)

A/M Drawing Number 1117/45 RAF Ashbourne – Dispersed Sites, Record Site Plan (RAF Museum, Hendon)

PRO AIR 29/679 RAF Ashbourne – Operations Record Book (National Archives, Kew, Surrey).

Anon (1975) Aviation News: *Aircraft Accident Summary*. 4/13, 11th December, 1975, p.3.

Barras, M. B. (2006) *Air of Authority - A History of RAF Organisation.* http://www.rafweb.org/Index.htm

Bowyer, C. (1984) *Bristol Blenheim.* Ian Allan Ltd, London.

Bowyer, M. J. F. & Rawlings, J. D. R. (1979) *Squadron Codes 1937 – 57.* Patrick Stephens Ltd, Cambridge.

Brew, A. (2nd ed., 1998) *Boulton Paul Aircraft.* Budding Books.

Brookes, R. J. (2003) *Nottinghamshire & Derbyshire Airfields in the Second World War.* Countryside Books, Newbury, Berkshire.

Giddings, M. L. (1984) *Royal Air Force Ashbourne.* Colerne Debden Publishing, Ashbourne.

Hall, A. W. & Taylor, E. (1972) *Avro Anson: Marks I, III, IV & X.* Almark Publications.

Halley, J. J. (1980) *The Squadrons of the Royal Air Force.* Air Britain (Historians) Ltd, Tonbridge, Kent.

Halley, J. J. (1983) *Royal Air Force Aircraft WA100 – WZ999.* Air-Britain (Hostrians) Ltd, Tonbridge, Kent.

Halley, J. J. (1985) *Royal Air Force Aircraft AA100 – AZ999.* Air-Britain (Historians) Ltd, Tonbridge, Kent.

Halley, J. J. (1987) *Royal Air Force Aircraft DA100 – DZ999.* Air-Britain (Historians) Ltd, Tonbridge, Kent.

Halley, J. J. (1989) Royal *Air Force Aicraft HA100 – HZ999.* Air-Britain (Historians) Ltd, Tonbridge, Kent.

Halley, J. J. (1991) Royal *Air Force Aircraft LA100 – LZ999.* Air-Britain (Historians) Ltd, Tonbridge, Kent.

Halpenny, B. B. (1st ed., 1981) *Action Stations 2: Military Airfields of Lincolnshire & the East Midlands.* Patrick Stephens Ltd, London.

Jefford, C. J. Wing Commander (2nd ed) (2001) *RAF Squadrons.* Airlife, Shrewbury.

Lecaplan, B. (2005) *A Brief History of N° 38 Wing and N° 38 Group.* http://www.raf38group.org

Neville, L. (2002) *Return to Buxton: 28 MU, RAF Harpur Hill.* Woodcote Press, Ambleside, Cumbria.

Morgan, E. B. & Shacklady, E (1987) *Spitfire: The History.* Key Publishing, Stamford.

Richards, D. (3rd ed, 2001) *RAF Bomber Command in the Second World War: The Hardest Victory.* Penguin Books, London.

Robertson, B. (3rd ed) (1979) *British Military Aircraft Serials 1911 – 1979.* Patrick Stephens Ltd, London.

Smith, D. J. (1st ed., 1981) *Action Stations 3: Military Airfield of Wales & the North West*. Patrick Stephens Ltd, London.

Smith, D. J. (1st ed., 1989) *Britain's Military Airfields 1939-45*. Patrick Stephens Ltd, London.

Streetly, M. (1987) *Confound and Destroy*. Macdonald & Jane's, London.

Sturtivant, R. C. (1987) *The History of Britain's Military Training Aircraft*. Haynes Publishing, Yeovil.

Sturtivant, R. C. (1988) *The Anson File*. Air Britain (Historians) Ltd, Tonbridge, Kent.

Tapper, O. (1988) *Armstrong Whitworth Aircraft Since 1913*. Putnam.

Weeks, J. (1978) *Assault from the Sky: A History of Airborne Warfare*. Westbridge Books, Newton Abbot, Devon.

Willis, S. & Holliss, B. (1987) *Military Airfields in the British Isles 1939 – 1945 (Omnibus Edition)*. Enthusiasts Publications, Sherrington, Bucks.

Wixey, K. (1997) *Forgotten Bombers of the Royal Air Force*. Arms & Armour Press, London.